A WORD IN YOUR EAR

A WORD IN YOUR EAR

by

IVOR BROWN

JONATHAN CAPE
THIRTY BEDFORD SQUARE
LONDON

FIRST PUBLISHED SEPTEMBER 1942
SECOND IMPRESSION SEPTEMBER 1942
THIRD IMPRESSION OCTOBER 1942
FOURTH IMPRESSION NOVEMBER 1942
FIFTH IMPRESSION MARCH 1943
SIXTH IMPRESSION FEBRUARY 1944

JONATHAN CAPE LTD.   30 BEDFORD SQUARE, LONDON
AND 91 WELLINGTON STREET WEST, TORONTO

BOOK
PRODUCTION
WAR ECONOMY
STANDARD

THIS BOOK IS PRODUCED IN COM-
PLETE   CONFORMITY   WITH   THE
AUTHORIZED ECONOMY STANDARDS

PRINTED IN GREAT BRITAIN IN THE CITY OF OXFORD
AT THE ALDEN PRESS
PAPER MADE BY JOHN DICKINSON & CO. LTD.
BOUND BY A. W. BAIN & CO. LTD.

WORDS UPON WORDS

THE book which follows is an anthology of words. Anthologies
of prose and verse abound: but there is, I think, no such volume of
their raw material, which is words. If it be deemed pleasant to
gather bouquets of the former, why should the latter be left only in
the cold storage of the lexicon? The phrase 'flowers of speech' has
been unhappily applied with jocosity and even contempt to what
Mr. Wells's Mr. Polly so nicely entitled 'verboojuice'. But
'flowers of speech' is an exact description of an anthology of
words. Words, like flowers, have colour and bloom and aroma.
They are to the writer as paint to the artist and, while they have
been scientifically examined and listed and defined without cease
by learned men and lexicographers, they merit also the purely
affectionate approach of the collector who assembles his favourites
in order to gratify both his sense of meaning and his sense of beauty
in verbal shape and sound.

My method has been simple, personal, and vagrant. I have
noted and collected the words which caught my fancy during my
casual war-time reading, much of it re-reading of half-forgotten
acquaintances and of abiding friends. I have not gone exploring
for strange and striking terms. Had I chosen to do so, I could have
made a whole anthology of rareties merely by raking the surface
of Urquhart, Burton, and Ben Jonson. Once attracted by a word
and looking into antecedents and parentage, I have grubbed in the
Dictionary. But is grub a fair description? Scarcely. One is
dealing with the flowers as well as with their native earth. Dictionaries are green and blossoming pastures, wherein any fancier of
curious and delightful things can meander contentedly for days.

In my selection I have made no rules. What pleased, was noted:
what noted, sifted: what survived the sieve, is here. I have in most
cases quoted one passage or more in which the word appeared and
gave pleasure. I have quoted freely because words, like precious

stones and cut flowers, depend upon their grouping and the choice of neighbours. They may be strange or beautiful or amusing in isolation, but they will be doubly so when an author of judgment has put them in the right company.

Strange, beautiful, amusing — I have made my pick for all sorts of reasons. I have not barred American or Scottish or dialect words: I have included archaisms and obsolete terms as well as modern slang. No rule but personal relish has guided me. In general, I have chosen words which I would like to see employed more often or more accurately, rescued from neglect and restored to their appropriate power.

My taste, it will at once be seen, is catholic. I like the short and Saxon: I like the long and Latin. Domestic or alien, farmyard or courtly, all that has distinctive quality goes into the bowl. So long as a writer knows what he means and can express it, he can delight me as a Puritan stylist, with his English as close-cropt as his hair, or he can affect the laces and the ribbons of language and display all the panache of a Cavalier: he can be classical or romantic, urbane as Pope or rustic as John Clare. The abomination in the use of words is obscurity. This tiresome quality may be caused by a pose, as in the earlier work of sprouting genius, or by a brain that works too fast and cascades its clauses and images in a torrent, as in some later work of Shakespeare, or it may be the result of muddled thinking. Be it affectation or incompetence, it is a more common and more afflicting nuisance than is pomposity, which suits its own epochs and has its own enjoyable grandeur, as shows upon a stage may be portentous, even vulgarly massive, and yet somehow likeable. I have read that Mr. Winston Churchill, who can be florid as well as tremendous with his pen, based his style on a young addiction to Gibbon and Macaulay. There is a case for the sounding period to suit the high, substantial theme.

In a Country Churchyard

An easy way to study the ups-and-downs of language and the different tastes of different generations in the use of words is

6

to take one's gentler exercise in churches and churchyards, which are indeed the marble-index of a nation's mind voyaging in strange seas of valedictory emotion. This is a pastime open to all and one leading to serene and not altogether melancholy places.

The church and its tombs are a chronicle of style and state of mind. As such they may be depressing because they reveal, at least during the last hundred years, a steady decline of taste in material, in sentiment, in diction, and in lettering. The oldest stones have a native modesty: their grey simplicity emerges without fuss: they seem to grow as naturally as the daisies in the grass beside them. Even when fresh-cut they cannot have been out of place or flashily demonstrative, as are the sepulchres of alien marble which came into a later vogue. The words which they carry have a quiet dignity, and so has the lettering of these sincere and tranquil tributes. Men in those days were allowed to die: death need not be disguised with larger words.

True, the eighteenth century had its pomps; it would put into an English village the amplitude of a Roman gesture and bid farewell to a Georgian Squire with an Augustan flourish. But there was style in the gesture, and, after all, our culture came very largely by way of Rome. The lover of words will forgive the pleasing classical rotundity and even delight in the fine formality of a dismissive phrase. Recently in a church of the Shakespeare country, to which I was the more attracted because so many of its dead were called by the name of Lively, I found a tablet upon the wall in honour of a young Georgian doctor's skill. By his art and science, it said, 'He prolonged the lives of others to lament his own dissolution'. The compliment may or may not be just; the phrasing is certainly perfect.

A touch of eighteenth-century scepticism crept in later when the memorial tablet added, 'He was removed, we trust, to immortality'. The potentially sardonic 'we trust' would not have been admitted in an age of real faith. The inscription concluded with conventional lines in heroic couplets.

7

> For thus Religion softly murmurs peace
> And bids the sorrows of the mourners cease.

Any quick schoolboy could churn this out by the page. But it has an atmosphere: it marches with the phrasing of the prose and the graving of the sentiments.

During the eighteenth century, according to my churchyard observations, people were allowed, quite simply, to die. Towards the end of that period they begin to 'depart this life'. That is a fuller term, but there is no evasion about it. All this time the valedictory compliments paid to these departed have a classical dignity on the more august sepulchres and a native good sense on the humbler stones. But about the year 1830 everything goes. It has often astonished me how sudden and all-inclusive was the collapse of taste. In a churchyard you notice no gradual decay, but a complete break.

The craft of Journalism, like that of epitaphy, employed at that period a sounding vocabulary and a great sense of cadence. There were space and leisure for the ample phrase and this magniloquence was to be discovered as much in a local sheet as in one of the more august London journals. In a bar-parlour in a remote Derbyshire dale I once noticed on the wall a cutting from a local paper. It was an obituary notice, written in the early nineteenth century about a gamekeeper who had become a centenarian and had executed some high feats of agility and endurance even when he was reaching three figures. It was written of his habits — I must quote from memory —

> Until the age of sixty he consumed but one gallon of malt liquor a day: but later he began to drink plentiful, which he found both agreeable to his constitution and an abiding comfort to himself.

Such prose employs no rare words, but it patterns the familiar terms to a noble surge of sound. The modern form of farewell to such a veteran of the chase and tankard would probably be some mean string of clichés, far less candid and without the sap of feeling or the dignity of phrase.

The historian of word-usage notes that in a year or two everything is spoiled. The classical grandeur is softened and turned sentimental. The calamity happened round about 1830. Simplicity vanishes, as well as the stately and sonorous rhythm. People no longer die, like Adam: they pass over, they go home, they are carried to rest, they fall asleep, they are removed to the divine bosom, or whisked to other celestial and possibly embarrassing niches. Anything but the plain fact of death. Their virtues are no longer stated with any regard for truth: the dead are all possessed of moral excellence beyond belief and their village must have been a communion of very tiresome saints. The epitaphic English becomes affected, ornate, and odious. Humbug, no doubt, was always with us. But now a particularly florid humbug has arrived. One wanders from sepulchre to sepulchre whose inscriptions suggest that Chadband has been burying a Tite Barnacle or that Podsnap has said 'Vale' to Veneering. The vulgarity is general and affects the quantity and quality of commemorative stone as well as the lettering and the language upon it. The churchyard, which used to be a piece of English country, grey and green, now glitters hideously with Italian marble.

Verboojuice

There is no reason why the long and weighty word should be a bad one. The craving for such mental implements is natural. The lad who wants the biggest missile in the biggest catapult is like a writer in the flush of youth. Marlowe's 'mighty line' was just such a weapon. To make a thundering noise, to use pen and lungs to the full, is an irresistible temptation to young nations as to young people. There seems to be no slow evolution of artistic skill. The cave-men painters emerged supreme at the start. Their animal murals are immediate masterpieces. So with language and poetry. The Greek epic arises, like Aphrodite from the wine-dark sea, complete in beauty and elaborate in eloquence. But not eloquent only in the simple style of mariners' song or peasant fable. It is rhetorical, verbose, many-syllabled song. The earliest Greek poetry has a treasury of long, large, musical phrases. The insurgent genius of the race reveals the young and lusty appetite for glorious and gigantic words. 'Poluphlois-boisterous Homer of old!'

It continually happens. Boyhood loves to use its lung-power. Mr. Wells's Mr. Polly, that Boy Eternal of English democracy, revelled, as I said, in 'sesquipeddle verboojuice'. He was behaving like William Shakespeare before him. Shakespeare began with the 'taffeta phrases, silken terms precise' of the modish Euphuism and proceeded to the terrific verbal detonations of his battle-pieces in the Histories, in which his munitions were an unquenchable gift of metaphor and a colossal vocabulary. In his major tragedies he still splashed freely in the 'verboojuice', while discovering the full powers of simplicity. *King Lear* contains magic of both kinds, spilling cataracts and hurricanoes, sulphurous fires and oak-cleaving thunderbolts as fitly on the horrid heath as it sheds the simplest tears over the corpses on the soil of Kent. Lear fooled away his kingdom with as much waste of noble words as of ignoble temper: then died to the sad, slow music of humanity, which was as native to his withering as to Wordsworth's thoughts at Tintern Abbey.

Long words only become offensive when they are also tired and dull. Who would have the dialogue between Hamlet and his father's Ghost written out in words of one syllable? Who would confine Othello to a lackey's lingo or have Hotspur speak only for the ears of modern Tottenham? But enjoyment of 'verboojuice', the grand 'sesquipeddle' stuff, does not excuse the dreary prolixity of our own time, as it is splashed across the pages of official forms, reports, propaganda, and Governmental scripts of all kinds. In loathing this I am a good constituent of Mr. A. P. Herbert, whose fight for decent English has properly befitted the Parliamentary representative of Oxford University. But it was not a total victory and much remains for tears.

A Journey in Jargantua

In our time the official has created a language, a fearsome and ponderous dialect which I once christened the Barnacular in memory of the Circumlocution Office and its Tite Barnacle Controllers. But let us be fair to the Civil Servant: the official is not the only dealer in officialese. There is in this country an enormous and semi-official bureaucracy which deals in social welfare and all manner of educational and uplifting matters. It is rapidly developing a jargon of its own, a semi-officialese which is even worse than anything to be discovered within the envelopes marked O.H.M.S. It has the pomposity of style favoured by the self-important Business Man mixed up with the pretentiousness of those who dabble vaguely in Social Sciences. While the Government afflicts us with the Barnacular, the Uplifters and Welfarists are assaulting us with the similar horrors of their Jargantuan.

Let me quote a sentence from a document of this type. It was not composed by any member of the much-abused Civil Service. It is sad to think that it was concerned with a form of education, and, since it was composed by one of our would-be educators, we may well shudder at the notions of English speech that are now to be instilled. When the author of this piece of prose wished to say 'How the young now live' he put it thus: 'Material descriptive of conditions at present governing the lives of under-twenties (cross-sectional).' He thus used twenty-eight syllables instead of five and two or three lines instead of half a line at a time when saving of print and paper was said to be most necessary. Whenever he intended to talk of 'sundry people' he had to write 'a cross-section of the community'. Indeed, this word 'cross-section' so much went to his head (because of its length and Latinity) that he even talked of a family as a 'cross-section of the community', although that is exactly what the family is not, if the word has any point whatever.

So it ran on. The cumbrous phrase was invariably preferred to the simple. Are we to sympathize with the young? Certainly, if we are good citizens. But need this be called 'Self-identification with the experience, interests and problems of other young people (over a wide range) and also with their points of view and emotional attitudes'? One begins to believe that a man who can write this stuff would rather eat his own typewriter than call a feeling a feeling. It must be an 'emotional attitude'. Another tiresome habit in which such folk revel is the use of an adjective as a noun, presumably because it sounds unusual and therefore imposing. They have to lengthen everything, but you would think it enough to call an order a direction. No, they have to make it 'a directive', just as reforms have to be 'correctives'.

Needless to say, the word 'reaction' occurred constantly. 'Bringing correctives to bear upon reactions to war-time experience' probably means something. But, being an innocent abroad in this land of Jargantua, I would not care to say what. However, I am a poor hand at this whole business of spinning syllables. I have always preferred 'naughty children' to 'juvenile delinquents' and 'mend' to the now universal 'recondition'. What parent ever asked his boy not to be 'delinquent', or told him to 'recondition' his manners? I would rather 'start a talk and sum up' than 'promote discussion and synthesize the various categories of reaction'. But I am beginning in sorrow to believe that there are few on my side. Certainly the War Office is in the opposite camp and strongly entrenched in Jargantua. Why do its 'spokesmen' never call a ridge a ridge but always an 'escarpment'? Would these same fellows, if proposing a peace-time picnic, suggest some neighbouring 'escarpment' as a scene for lunch? Old-fashioned regiments and companies now seem to be always 'operational units'. 'Operational' has become a very operative word.

How does this Jargantuan stuff come to get written? The composers of it have, as a rule, had university educations. Were they permitted (or even encouraged) by their tutors to employ this mess of pointless and polysyllabic classicism instead of plain, brief English? It certainly is the case that, once you intimate to a student that the proper study of mankind is man, he immediately concludes that the proper English for setting down his views about the lives of his fellows is that which no normal Englishman ever did speak in actual life and, let us hope, never will.

Not long ago there was a broadcast about war-time on the farm which was delivered by Wiltshire cowmen, shepherds, and labourers in a natural way with an agreeable burr to their speech and a sensible reliance upon the vocabulary of the village. But suddenly, in the midst of it, one cowman said, 'We, with our depleted staff . . .' instead of 'We, with many away'.

Depleted staff! It is the very hall-mark of officialese, with its Latinity and its use of a formal and imposing word, staff, instead of the simpler 'hands' or 'men'. We need not suppose that the cowman wished to be imposing and to seem a fine, book-learned speaker at the 'mike'. He might have used the phrase any day at his own fireside, because words of this kind come pouring over the air and are inserting themselves into the common talk 'unbeknownst', as they used to say. The Ancient Greeks had a nice phrase about the man who 'escaped his own notice becoming drunk'. So nowadays we escape our own notice becoming verbose. All the Ministries encourage this vice. Why, for example, say of a certain food that it is 'in short supply' when all you mean is that it is scarce? I have not yet heard a housewife tell her husband that eggs are 'in short supply' this week, but that, like 'depleted staff' upon the farmer's lips, may come.

Some of Our Conquerors

The war, through the power it gives to bureaucracy and to the industrialists turned public administrators, will certainly add to our language — or rather inflate it. The tendency of such people is always to prefer a new and heavy word to an old and short one. In doing that they are following a habit particularly dear to our time, that is, to take the noun belonging to a verb and then to turn that noun into another and a longer verb. The most absurd and offensive example of this is the use of the word 'to decision'. 'Decide' is not nearly swollen enough for the swollen-headed Napoleon of a Film Corporation. 'Have you decisioned this?' he inquires, with a happy illusion of appearing the Educated Man. The American up-lifters have turned 'inspiring' into the ghastly 'inspirational', and their opposites, the American gangsters, who are supposed to talk quick, 'peppy' language, are often as long-winded and Latin-loving as any. They use 'to suspicion' instead of 'to suspect' (see James Cain's brilliantly horrible story *The Postman Always Rings Twice*). Nowadays the motor-trade has made a silly verb on similar lines, 'to service'.

There is, of course, a good case for keeping the language fluid and receptive. Mr. H. L. Mencken justly points out that Shakespeare and Ben Jonson enriched English frequently by their use of nouns as verbs. What an excellent word, for example, is the Shakespearean 'to spaniel' — that is, to follow in a flattering, fawning way, as the officers under Antony 'spaniel'd him at heels'! But such a trick is quite different from the abominable malpractice of taking the abstract noun made from a verb and then using that as a verb — e.g., 'to decision'. Mr. Mencken does indeed dismiss as silly such a usage as that, but he notes with satisfaction the official usage of 'to contact' in his country and the American Navy's acceptance of the verb 'to message'. Perhaps these are justified. There is no word which covers approach by telephone, letter, and speech, and 'contact' and 'message', used as verbs, are self-explanatory and concise.

He gently dismisses 'to signature' as 'redundant'. It is, in fact, as odious a waster of breath and space as 'to decision', since it adds two more syllables to a perfectly good word of one. That ridiculous habit of making additions, in order to seem important, is to be seen again in the film trade's use of the word 'to author' instead of 'to write'. 'Finalize' for 'end' is a new horror of this kind. The object here is to have a Latin word of two or three syllables instead of a Saxon word of one, the notion being that the simpletons to whom the films appeal will be vastly impressed by polysyllabic 'blurbs'.

Many words which were scolded on their first appearance have since lived on to acquire a good character as well as to perform a good function. Mr. Mencken quotes 'belittle', first used by Thomas Jefferson in 1787 and violently derided in London, and mentions as others once tabu in orthodox quarters but now accepted, freely employed, and allotted dictionary status, 'influential, handy, mileage, dutiable, lengthy, to advocate, to legislate, to progress, and to locate'. 'To progress' is, perhaps, the most interesting of this list. It is a verb formed from a noun, but it is not long or clumsy. But in a short time an eminent Film 'Executive' will dismiss it as paltry and insufficient for the trumpeting of his forward-looking purposes and proceed to regard 'progression' as a more imposing verb. 'The fact that we have finalized a Six Months All-America Conference on Consumer Reaction to Art Pictures and have decisioned to create an All-Star Motion-Picture in Glorious, Glamorous Stereoscopic Technicolour, authored and signatured by Nelson Schmalzheimer and planned to run for eight hours with only two intermissions, indicates the rate of progressioned exhibitioning envisaged by Super-Superlative Pictures.' Such writing is increasingly with us.

Britain seems now to have swallowed and digested the American use of 'executive' as a noun. Being long and Latin, it is a natural favourite with those who so learnedly call a lift an 'elevator' and bid you 'operate' instead of work it. There was a time when American could fairly claim to be a 'snappy' language. But now it prefers prolixity to 'pep'. Have not its 'bosses' all become 'Executives'? Incidentally, 'an Executive' for a man who decides, a boss, is not only pompous but incorrect. Executive action is that which carries out somebody else's orders, a humble matter of following out, which is what the word originally meant. Our own Civil Service rightly grades its Administrative Class above its Executive Class.

How far American has been overwhelmed by this passion for classicism is revealed by the holy man of Harlem, who has called himself in turn The Messenger, Major J. Devine, Father Divine, and finally, and simply, God. This celestial coon, who has an immense following, bids the flock 'contact me harmoniously' and assures them that he is 'visibilating and tangibilating' their fondest imaginations. The gentleman may act as a very fine influence on the ethics and happiness of Harlem, but he is plainly doing the American language no good at all. The Negroes who once made their spirituals out of Bible English were fortunate to avoid this gas-bag stuff of the new evangelism at large in Jargantua.

The itch for length in diction becomes continually more powerful. Take the case of the final, the usually unnecessary, preposition. When I was a boy we checked figures: next we checked them up: now we 'check up on' them. Test and try once sufficed. Now everybody 'tries out' or 'tests out' this or that. Shall our cricketers have 'Test-Out' Matches? People no longer win. They 'win through' or even 'win out'. Vilest of all, perhaps, are 'face up to' for 'face' and 'meet up with', which says nothing more than 'meet.'

The Quick and the Dead

Words, like all other creatures, can be worked to death. The more we write and print — talking is hardly so lethal — the more words do we reduce to weaklings and even to corpses. What happens is that the words which are supposed to be specially picturesque or exciting appear so often that they are taken for granted. The image behind them ceases to be effective: they dwindle, despite their once great vigour and value, into the cliché class.

The first man, for example, to talk of a 'sickening thud', employed a vivid metaphor for acutely physical terror. But its success was its ruin. Every thud is now sickening and the idea of a fright producing actual nausea has quite gone. So with 'stony silence'. There are people who cannot use the word 'silence' without automatically prefixing 'stony'. What they mean by it they could not say. For stones are not notably silent. If struck, they clang. If trodden on, they make more noise than grass. If thrown, they produce 'sickening thuds'. Vegetable matter or cloth is much more quiet stuff than any mineral. Why not say 'a grassy' or 'a velvet' silence? It would be more accurate and more effective. Stony silence is really as dead as a neolithic flint.

I do not propose to wander further into the gigantic forest of Cliché. It has been carefully explored and charted by that active lexicographer, Mr. Eric Partridge, whose *Dictionary of Clichés* is a wonderful graveyard of the good phrase killed by kindness. For most clichés are tremendously vivid when they are born. Consider such a phrase as 'beggaring description'. It was a tremendous metaphor when first used by Shakespeare. Now it is valueless.

We should, however, observe one particular form of word-slaughter in the hope that we may occasionally rescue a nice term from this butchery. Journalism, pouring out its millions of words daily, is inevitably a murderer. In the game of word-making and word-taking it takes (and destroys) far more than it makes. What it takes nowadays is usually the short word, for the obvious reason that the formidable 'verboojuice' is of no use to those making up headlines for columns and captions for posters. Their business is to say as much as possible in the least possible space. Hence they seize on brevities, even if they happen to be antiques, such as 'slay' for murder or assassinate, 'parley' for conference or discussion, and 'key' for important. (In war-time everybody seems to be a key man, doing a key job, in a key town.) This cult of brevity may result in choices strangely unsuitable, such as lively for exciting when the subject is death. Thus a Trade Union Conference becomes on bills and headlines 'T.U. Parley' — well might a foreigner wonder who the fellow is — and a class-war riot is reported under 'Reds Slay Whites. Thousands Dead in Key Town. Lively Scenes'.

One of the words recently flattened out by the excessive attentions of journalism has been thrill, which is so much shorter than excitement or suspense. Thrill has had a specially hard time because it is the business of newspapers, especially in peace-time when things are dull, to discover excitements. If there is no news, news must be whipped up. Breakfast and supper without a ration of sensation are unthinkable. Therefore excitements are duly provided and, for sake of brevity, thrill is the chosen word. Pity the poor cricket-reporter sent to watch a dull game. Nothing whatever happens all day, but it is his job to record high lights and great deeds. At last, after hours of tedium, somebody misses a catch or is run out. Despairingly, he makes a feature of it. Next morning he sees that the sub-editor has headed his tale 'Thrills at Lord's'. Does this annoy spectators who had sat there all day swooning with boredom? Apparently not, but it infuriates me.

The unhappy history of 'thrill' is noted later in this book. So is that of glamour, a lovely victim of shocking misuse and constant over-work. Epic is another unfortunate. In the most humdrum times newspapers abound in 'Epic Struggles'. Do we not read 'Police Trail Bandit. Epic Chase', or 'Girl-Wife in Court. Epic Scenes'? We do, but the adjective, being dead, does not set us thinking of the major poets or of warriors spearing and spouting on the windy plains of Troy. Alas, poor Homer! He is not only caused to nod; he is totally floored. Any bit of nonsense can be 'epic' now, while some hiker's holiday outing may be absurdly dignified with the truly epic and honourable title of an 'Odyssey'.

That sort of thing is inevitable. When tools are blunted the best policy is to give them a rest. So, no doubt, with our words. If we could lay aside the thrills and glamours and the like for a very long period of repose, they might be able to return revived. But the life of words cannot be organized. The difficulty is to create suitable new words in societies which have been subjected to a formal education. For this education usually limits the creative capacity. Peasants make words easily — good, vigorous, picturesque words. But our urban and mechanical life is rarely inventive in this way: all its wits are going into its machines and so, apart from occasional bursts of slang-creation, it works with featureless abbreviations of long classical terms, like 'mike' for microphone, or else it does not even shorten at all but is loyal to the ponderous. It is queer that people so much concerned with speed as are motorists should be content with long and lumbering terms, such as limousine, accelerator, and carburettor, none of which is commonly shortened. Motors, as Mr. Osbert Sitwell has pointed out, entered this country as very odd, foreign contraptions which only some very odd creature like a foreigner could be supposed to understand. Hence the use of 'chauffeur', which has lingered on in our language, like hotel, chef, and valet. Perhaps some snobbery was at the back of this. The fact remains that the mechanization of our lives has weighted our English down far more than it has speeded it up. Compared with our ancestors we are a tongue-tied generation.

It is unfortunately true that people interested in words, which, as the vehicles of thought and feeling, are as vital to our lives as food and drink and fire and shelter, become unconsciously conservative. Many people instinctively resent new words and usages. That may be the product of an education which is so largely an immersion in traditional things. When any novelty of speech arrives, even a lively and serviceable novelty, there is certain to be strong protest. It is dismissed as a vulgar modernism, without much consideration as to the proper meaning of vulgar and the necessity of modern words for modern things. I hope that I shall never be caught condemning a good new word simply because it is new, but the virus of conservatism is powerful and one frequently finds oneself opposing what may turn out to be a valuable piece of creation.

In what follows far more will appear about old words than about new. My anthology has been made rather as a record of personal pleasures than as a weapon for linguistic reformers. I have amused myself with word-collection. But that does not indicate any lack of appetite for word-creation. Let us have new words in abundance, but not the kind of word which is merely an old and short and stout one made long and flabby. Why, for example, call a job an assignment?

Until our tongue has become fecund again we may profit by some revivals of the just word unjustly neglected. This anthology suggests a few which seem to merit a glorious resurrection. One profitable line of procedure would be to recover from America some of the good, simple words which the Pilgrim Fathers took in their cabin-trunks. American is either the best of English or the worst, the best when it preserves the vigour of the seventeenth century, the worst when it is mixing Social Science with 'inspirational' sentiments. The dabblers in matters of the Psyche have created a truly abominable 'psychologese', in which responses are always reactions, every sort of desire is a complex, and to be fond of mamma is inevitably called possession by a mother-fixation.

(So far has this nasty lingo permeated from the lecturer's dais to the common convention that nobody now asks me my opinion of this or that. It is always 'What is your reaction?') I have at hand a work composed by one of this School on *The Nature of the Soul* in which thought is always called opinionation, while the word integration appears in almost every paragraph, though I doubt whether the author knows what it means. Here is a powerful specimen of that gentleman's curious vocabulary and creed:

> And as for the fertilization of one soul-integration by another — look how *that* process is collectivized by the Article of Covenant governing External Synthesis. There we see provision for The Society of Life (the world's first seeding group) to enter into serious fertilizing relations with the appropriate external group. This is not a mere metaphor. The spirit of the seed is in it. It *is* fertilization. It *is* the road to unfoldment, in place of the stony integrations which lead to opposition of a hatefilled kind.

That is one sort of American English. But the English need not vaunt themselves. They have their own masters in this kind. The other sort is the sensible, concise Tudor English which uses 'beat it' for go. Ben Jonson's characters are to be discovered 'beating it' down the cobbled street. Sidewalk, again, which is seventeenth-century English, is a much better term than our pavement since it describes what it is meant to be, whereas pavement might mean any paved surface. It is astonishing how the modern American, not the modern English, usage turns up when one is reading the Elizabethans. When I play cards, my English friends talk of a pack. When I go to the pictures, the American gangsters ask for 'a deck of cards'. So, when he wanted a game, did Shakespeare — or who ever it was that wrote 3 *Henry VI*, v, 1.

> But, when he thought to steal the single ten,
> The king was slily fingered from the deck.

I am not suggesting that deck is a better word than pack, but merely citing a striking case of the emigrants' verbal luggage.

In addition to hinting at the need for revivals and reimportations, I may, I hope, persuade a few more people to be interested in words, whose oddity and beauty, whose strange parentage and exquisite aspects and rhythms make them excellent material for collectors. Man is an acquisitive animal and nearly everybody amasses and dotes upon something in addition to his grievances. The collecting tribe has applied itself to an extraordinary range of articles, ranging from eggs and orchids and butterflies to stamps and coins and walking-sticks. If the locks of hair and shoe-buckles of the great are meet for hoarding, what of their words, often the prime instruments of their power? If it is good to collect first editions, why not the stuff of which that precious print is made?

To be a collector of language is an innocent occupation. The snatchers and hoarders of birds' eggs and of flowers first create a scarcity, then hunt down the rareties (or, even worse, hire others to go marauding for them) and finally exterminate the beauty which they crave. To go a-fowling on the slopes of Helicon with those flashing, sounding beauties, the words, as coveted prize invades no rights and does no violence to life. To hunt words is to do no trespass. Rather does it keep or elicit good things for the common use and public pleasure instead of destroying them or making them scanty for a privy satisfaction. Words can be as rich to the senses as a Painted Lady, Purple Emperor, Bird of Paradise, and the most orchidaceous blooms of domestic marsh or alien jungle. Like coins in the purse and stamps on letters, which also men covet and collect, they serve a simple need. They throw colour on to paper and make music in the air. Words are wind and fire: but those are difficult articles to collect. They are also the seed of action and the blossom of thought, which are easier for the anthologist. I have found some words which are withering and deserve to recover their old strength and liveliness, others, more scarce, which are rising to power and merit that emergence. I have found, and hope to go on finding, the droll specimen and the thing of beauty. Readers of Shakespeare know to their great comfort that they are never finished with him. They turn to a passage which they had heard or read a thousand times; every syllable is stale: yet suddenly a new beauty leaps out from the famous and familiar lines. The English vocabulary, like Shakespeare its matchless employer and its giver of increase, has always some untapped or neglected mines of precious metal. It is the El Dorado of collectors.

ACKNOWLEDGEMENT

THE right to quote from copyright work is a matter teeming with legal complexity. Authors to whom I have appealed because I was quoting more than a phrase or a few lines have shown me the greatest kindness, and I would like to express my gratitude to Miss Bambridge, Mr. A. P. Watt, and Messrs. Methuen (in the matter of quoting from Rudyard Kipling), to Mr. Hilaire Belloc, to Mr. John Betjeman, to Mr. Edmund Blunden, to Messrs. Laurence Housman, Jonathan Cape, and the Society of Authors (in the matter of quoting from A. E. Housman), to Messrs. Macmillan (in the matter of quoting from Kipling and Ralph Hodgson), and to Mr. Siegfried Sassoon; also to Mr. Arthur Ransome for helpful suggestions.

ALLAY

ALLAY is a verb of richest variety. In its time it has signified a fine assortment and even confusion of meanings, to overthrow or to appease, to dilute wine or to lay on hounds. I have also found it as one of a covey of Elizabethan verbs proper to the serving and carving of meats. These verbs run like the famous nouns of assembly, a pride of lions, skulk of foxes, gaggle of geese, and so on. Robert May, author of *The Accomplisht Cook*, thus parades them:

> Lift that Swan; Rear that Goose; Dismember that Hern; Unbrace that Mallard; Unlace that Coney; Allay that Pheasant; Wing that Partridge; Display that Quail; Unjoynt that Bittern; Unlatch that Curlew; Break that Egript; Thigh that Woodcock.

One can imagine them rolled with a sonorous rapture on a Malvolio's tongue as he overlooked the ordering of his lady's table for a day of high entertainment. Sir Toby, too, would have gladly and imposingly commanded the allaying of a young roast pheasant.

ALOOF

ALOOF, to me a vividly expressive word, is a gift from the sea: it is derived from the nautical 'luffing', one of whose meanings is to get the windward side of your opponent in a race or battle. So aloof meant 'away to the windward', and then apart from or away in any sphere. Milton used it almost as a preposition, calling the sun 'alooff the vulgar constellations thick', and that implies the sense of pride and superiority which the word now so nicely carries. I owe to Mr. James Agate an admirable quotation from a wine-merchant's list, 'This claret is so distinguished as to be almost aloof'. There are always authors and artists to whom aloofness is a natural or a desirable and cultivated pose. They take to themselves the exquisite refinement of the vintage aforesaid. Milton's 'vulgar constellations thick' suggests the kind of stage-party which is called a galaxy. To be aloof at such a gathering admirably describes the faint participation of a literary gentleman who believes himself to be above such matters, say a Henry James bidden to a feast of that starry, but breezily benignant Music-hall companionage, The Water Rats.

ANIMATION

ANIMATE, for quicken, was known to Marlowe and Milton, but, rather strangely, unused by Shakespeare. In the eighteenth century it acquired a technical sense which has charm as well as pertinence. The various recognized antics and capers of a Harlequin in the pantomimes of the period were known as his several 'animations'. Great actors, like all great artists, have their various tricks, nowadays called technique, for obtaining their effects. In the case of so vivid an art as acting, it would be appropriate to preserve the word once so picturesquely bestowed on Harlequin. What playgoer does not know and relish the 'animations' of Sir Seymour Hicks?

ANNOY

COMMON enough surely, but weakened now by its restriction to personal vexation. Once it meant to harm or corrupt and was applied to all nuisances.

> As one who long in populous City pent
> Where Houses thick and Sewers annoy the Aire

is Milton's usage of annoy. There was wont to be a Jury of Annoyances to decide about such public pests as 'Houses thick and Sewers'. Nowadays the would-be solitary, who seeks to be lonely in the hills, finds the air 'annoyed' with aeroplanes, and we have all seen golfers, annoyed in our sense, who appeared to be most obviously annoying the turf.

24

ARRANT

ARRANT comes very trippingly off the tongue as an adjunct and aggravation of abuse. There is some real satisfaction in adding 'arrant' to one's description of a knave or rogue. The word has a curious history. It was a form of errant, which means vagrant or wandering, and it was thus especially applied to strolling thieves. Then, by a mistake as to the origin, an arrant thief was taken to mean a particularly guilty or shameless specimen, a very thievish thief. So arrant began to be put in front of any adjective, even a friendly one, to add to its weight. First we have arrant thief, i.e. wandering pilferer, then arrant scoundrel, i.e. a very wicked wretch with no suggestion of movement, and lastly, an arrant good fellow, stressing simply his genuine excellence. But arrant was best and most commonly used with opprobrious intention. Shakespeare's texts abound in arrant knaves, thieves, and whores. Was it arrant folly on our part to let it slip?

AWFUL

IN *Some Miseries of Human Life*, an admirable compilation of social calamities made by 'Samuel Sensitive and Timothy Testy', there is set down as one of the main horrors of a rural ride,

> Visiting an Awful Ruin, in the company of a Romp of one sex or a Hun of the other.

It is curious to discover this use of Hun, presumably as a boorish, uncultivated fellow, with the old and good use of Awful as awe-inspiring. No word has been more foully mishandled than the latter. Romp, for a chattering, facetious adult, instead of a turbulent child, seems to be another good thing lost.

BABBLE

BABBLE is descriptive of childish or senile babble. Dying Falstaff babbled of green fields as any babe of his food and trinkets. But babble is not a mean or ugly word and it is justly applied to the songs of birds, not merely to the cuckoo's prattle, as Wordsworth applied it, but to the master-singers themselves. Mr. Ralph Hodgson has invented the babble-wren; at least orthodox ornithology is ignorant of this voluble mite.

> There, sharp and sudden, there I heard —
> Ah! some wild, lovesick, singing bird
> Woke singing in the trees!
> The nightingale and babble-wren
> Were in the English greenwood then,
> And you heard one of these?

For Gerard Manley Hopkins the lark is a babbler,

> Not that the sweet-fowl, song-fowl needs no rest,
> Why hear him, hear him babble and drop down to his nest.

Inanimate things can be likewise vocal.

> The stripling Thames at Bablock Hythe

What a name for what a place! The water-music of the Upper River babbles in the memory of all who have loved Oxford.

BARKABLE

THE use of adjectives ending in -able is peculiar. They are usually passive, as in lovable, eatable, drinkable, and so on. But knowledgeable, which used to mean knowable, has of late been commonly employed to mean 'knowing'. This I took to be an affectation or a faulty modernism, until coming across such a word as barkable for able to bark, which is as old as the thirteenth century. Eileen Power quotes this exquisite passage from a treatise of that period on Estate Management.

> It profiteth the lord to have discreet shepherds, watchful and kindly, so that the sheep be not tormented by their wrath but

crop their pasture in peace and joyfulness; for it is a token of the shepherd's kindness if the sheep be not scattered abroad but browse around him in company. Let him provide himself with a good barkable dog and lie nightly with his sheep.

Was John Davidson's 'runnable stag' fit to be hunted or actively fleet? In either case it might be a cause of barkability.

BARNACULAR

T H I S will not be found in the dictionary and its inclusion is a piece of vanity. While writing once of the Tite Barnacles, the great clan of office-holders satirized by Dickens in *Little Dorrit*, I had reason to mention that they are habitually cited by modern journalism to mock the Civil Service. As a matter of fact, the whole point of the Dickensian attack is that the Barnacle clan had its clutches on everything, ruled and exploited all the services and professions, and expected to have the fattest pickings of Church, Law, Medicine, etc. as well as of the Government Departments. However, one of its chief fortresses was the Circumlocution Office and so the Barnacles have become especially associated with bureaucratic dalliance and pedantry and the issue of complicated forms composed in an abominable jargon. I have the greatest respect for the British Civil Service, which recruits and retains many of the best brains in the country, but I must confess to sharing Mr. A. P. Herbert's abhorrence of their 'officialese' English. This lingo I ventured to call 'The Barnacular'.

BEREAVE

A c o m m o n word and beautiful, which you can. if you are a strict zealot of etymology, trace back to Com. Teut., O. Teut., and O. Eng. origins and link up with vocables like 'bereafian'. Being no such zealot, I merely observe that to bereave meant to pill and rob before it meant to make orphans or remove kindred. I include it because it touches no line of poetry which it does not decorate. A. E. Housman explained how certain sounds and phrases gave him such a shiver of ecstasy that he dare not mutter them while shaving. Not so physically susceptible, I find many lines of his to work less like earthquakes and more like anodynes. When afflicted with the ugliness of things it is a comfortable exercise to murmur almost anything of Housman's, not least

> With the great gale we journey
>   That breathes from gardens thinned,
> Borne in the drift of blossoms
>   Whose petals throng the wind;
>
> Buoyed on the heaven-heard whisper
>   Of dancing leaflets whirled
> From all the woods that autumn
>   Bereaves in all the world.

I cannot, and would not, take a walk in October without at least the final couplet of this lovely noise some time upon my lips.

BLAZON

THE whole peacock world of tabards and trumpets is blazoned in a single word. Blazon begins as a shield or banner, heraldically marked, and then comes to mean a description of such things: at last, a description or report of anything. As a term for tidings it has the full sonority of powerful brass. The Ghost of Hamlet's father, having threatened to 'harrow up the soul' with his news of life beyond the grave, remembers that such hair-raising information is not for the living.

> But this eternal blazon must not be
> To ears of flesh and blood.

This is, as I interpret it, a magnificently condensed phrase to signify report of the long hereafter. George Russell used blazoned in the

commoner sense in a quatrain of uncommon quality in his lines
'On behalf of Some Irishmen not Followers of Tradition'.

> No blazoned banner we unfold —
> One charge alone we give to youth,
> Against the sceptred myth to hold
> The golden heresy of truth.

Shakespeare was fond of blazon. Cassio calls Desdemona 'One that
excels the quirks of blazoning pens'. Words dear to the richest
wordman of them all must surely command the general affection.

BLIMPISH

WILL blimp and blimpish survive? (I prefer the adjective to the
noun.) The great cartoonist, Low, drew on the military balloon
for his Colonel and we may draw on that notable walrus for our
symbol of rubicund pomp and large, preposterous folly. Blimpish
goes with a way of life, which has not been lacking in good looks.
The Spa, the promenade, the croquet-lawns, the Club with its bald
domes of Anglo-Indian silence sunk sleepily in leather arm-chairs —
for these blimpish is no mere word of contempt. I recommend it
to Mr. John Betjeman, whose lighter muse is so happy among the
palings and balconies of the Victorian Colonel's paradise, where
my own boyhood was spent.

> Shall I forget the warm marquee
> And the general's wife so soon,
> When my son's colleger[1] acted as tray
> For an ice and a macaroon,
> And distant carriages jingled through
> The stuccoed afternoon?

He wrote of Cheltenham. To call its region of Pittville 'blimpish'
would be to honour the adjective, for Pittville is a charming model
of early nineteenth century town-planning, blimpish of old, and

[1] Mortar-board.

possibly still, in its personnel, but for a century benign to the eye and offering to the leisurely observer a gracious calendar of 'stuccoed afternoons'.

BLITZ

BLITZ-KRIEG, the lightning war, means something when war is suddenly declared or made. To talk of 'blitz-krieg' when a war has been going on for several years is mere nonsense. But the British seized the word 'blitz' because of its expressive likeness to blast and applied it to bombing. Bomb evidently struck the average mind as too weak a term except when a lonely missile fell. A large attack needed a larger word and 'blitz', most acceptable because of its brevity to composers of newspaper headlines, was welcomed. It is certainly more descriptive to the British mind than the 'strafe' of the last war. 'A blasted area' is equivocal to us. 'Blitzed' now is definite and painfully picturesque. The word may survive the dreadful occasion of its birth. Brevity, as I noted, is on its side, but that may result in its being over-worked before long (see the note on 'Thrill'). Meanwhile it goes with a bang.

BLOWEN

THIS, with its similar blowze, is one of the enormous list of English words for a coarse woman. But, according to Mr. W. L. Hanchant, editor of *The Newgate Garland*, it was first of all a blown-up type of person, 'any showy or flaunting woman, but finally a prostitute only, in contradistinction to joiner, a term of friendship applied to a fancy girl'. Joiner is a simply and sweetly descriptive term, which might be more widely remembered and employed. Blowze, which Herrick liked, also tells its story well. Blowen, in its original sense of a puffed-up, pretentious creature, with its inevitable suggestion of some physical grossness and wheezy flatulence as well, is the best of all. No steady supporter of the tavern can have passed his life without meeting many a blowze (in the public bar) and many a blowen (in the saloon).

BOOBY

BOOBY appears to be the fruit of a victory. It came in from Spain soon after the Armada and a fine, heavy dolt the booby is. Dryden, in one of his dramatic prologues, denounced 'the booby faces in the pit'. To us now the word savours of the nursery and belongs rather to the previous generation. But I can imagine it making an effective return into high politics. 'The petulant boobies of the Opposition'. Bunyan used it well of the tiresome, repetitive cuckoo.

> Thou booby, says't thou nothing but Cuckoo?

This is even better than A. E. Housman's

> The cuckoo shouts at nothing all day long.

The cuckoo may be sly enough in evading its parental cares, but proclaims itself, by lumbering flight and monotony of speech, true booby.

BOSKY

BOSKY naturally became an exile when the Tennysonian school of minstrelsy was broken up. True it is that bosky and boskage adorned many abominable verses in school-magazines, verses written in the odious lingo which proclaimed of sunrise that

> Phoebus hath clomb.

But bosky, a straight derivation from the Italian bosco, is a sensible word for wooded. England has abundant tangles of bracken and briar, bush and tree, which are most admirably described as bosky. In a handsome part of the Midlands, a westerly ridge of Staffordshire overlooking Shropshire, a region which has memories especially sacred for devotees of the House of Stuart, is Boscobel of the historic hiding-place and royal oak. Boscobel is simply a verbal importation from Italy, and means the lovely woodland. It is certainly a lovely word and should move us to grant to bosky the restitution of its ancient dignity and favour.

ELSEWHERE Milton's nice use of brag, in relation to physical grace, 'Beauty is Nature's brag and must be shown', is quoted. Since brag became a game of cards in which bluff was the chief element, this might be deemed a prophetic reference to strip-poker. Brag means a challenge as well as a boast and, as an adjective, lively. Garrick, in one of his many and fearsome Odes to Shakespeare, called him a 'Wag ever brag' (See note on Wag.) Shakespeare used brag in our sense and called Caesar's Veni, vidi, vici, a 'thrasonical brag'.

Bragless occurs at the end of that mint of strange words, *Troilus and Cressida*. Here is the passage:

DIOMEDE	The bruit is Hector's slain by Achilles.
AJAX	If it be so, yet bragless let it be;
	Great Hector was a man as good as he.
AGAMEMNON	March patiently along. Let one be sent
	To pray Achilles see us at our tent.
	If in his death the gods have us befriended,
	Great Troy is ours and our sharp wars are ended.

A modern Dick Whittington could scarcely do worse on Boxing Night. That Shakespeare wrote most of *Troilus and Cressida* is powerfully stamped upon the play's sour heart. But some of this rhymed stuff must surely have been taken over from, or vamped up by, another. Whoever wrote it obviously was not feeling very brag.

BROWNED OFF

NOT much Service slang became general speech during the first two years of the Greater War. 'Browned off', meaning bored, was an exception. I would like to think that it referred to the hue of the tired autumnal foliage. In that case it is the modern equivalent of Macbeth's decline into the sere, the yellow leaf. More probably it is a kitchen metaphor. To 'do brown', i.e. cheat, apparently comes from the notion of an ample roasting, which raises an interesting point. Why should the kindly craft of cookery be so ill thought of and applied to the forging of accounts and robbery of men? I like to regard 'browned off' as a trope from the October garden: no doubt I sentimentally delude myself.

BUMBASTE

BOMBAST, which is now used exclusively in this form and for a swollen kind of speech, is much more persuasive in its old spelling and might have retained its old meaning. Bumbaste was cotton-stuff used for stuffing garments and the heavily-quilted Tudor folk were bombastic indeed: still more so, James I, who bumbasted himself all over and wore immensely padded clothes in order to defeat the dreaded assassin's dagger. The word was then common as a verb. Greene accused the 'prentice Shakespeare of 'bumbasting' blank verses and Heywood wrote of plays bumbasted out with all manner of noisy irrelevance and mummerish titivations. He boasted his own austerity.

> A Strange Play you are like to have, for know
> We use no Drum, nor Trumpet, nor Dumbe Show:
> No Combate, Marriage, not so much to-day
> As Song, Dance, Masque to bumbaste out a play.

In the same way Shakespeare spoke of certain kinds of wit as 'The bumbaste and the lining of the time.' Our bombasine, a magnificent word considering the type of lady once addicted to this fabric, comes from the same origin, and might often with point have kept the old spelling. This leads to the further and scholastic usage of bumbaste, 'to beat the posteriors'.

CANTLE

THIS, for segment or portion, a thing cut, seems to have pined away from usage since Charles Lamb employed it. Shakespeare knew it and enjoyed its superior dignity and sonority. 'Part of the world' would not be much, but, when Antony's lieutenant says of his commander's dalliance,

> The greater cantle of the world is lost
> With very ignorance: we have kissed away
> Kingdoms and provinces,

the passionate squandering takes on imposing bulk. So there is a verb, to cantle, for cut; also a cantlet, for a tiny slice. Our restaurants would sound more richly did we but command 'a cantle of that pie'. Sliver is rare now for slice and rightly, for it is an ugly word. Let us keep cantle instead. Mention of slices reminds me of an old Scottish lady, described in a book of memories by J. J. Bell. When asked to take food at tea-time, she would at first decline and then accept what she called 'just a sensation of cake'.

CARAVEL

IT is odd that, while boating and sailing have so beautified the waters, they have so little adorned our language. Galleon was fine, but the smaller craft, gigs and brigs, sloops and schooners, cutters, frigates and pinnaces, yachts and yawls, are simply not good enough for the exquisite forms which they have represented. And as for our river-sports, canoe may pass, but skiff and punt and dinghy are deplorable. Why did we never promote coracle from the primitive tub that it was to serve our modern needs? Why, above all, did we let go the caravel, which sails with proper grace through the pages of Hakluyt and is occasionally remembered by our poets when dealing with the ancient mariner? Sir John Squire's sonnet 'There was an Indian' ends finely with the vision of the frightened aboriginal, who,

> His lips gone pale, knelt low behind a stone,
>   And stared, and saw, and did not understand,
>   Columbus's doom-burdened caravels
>   Slant to the shore, and all their seamen land.

Caravel may be somewhat alien, but a wise Imperialism would have seized and kept it.

CHEVISANCE

MR. HAROLD NICOLSON has pointed out that most of the Elizabethan flowers, which wave and glisten in the lyrics of the time, are still with us. But what has become of Chevisance and likewise of Pawnce which Spenser sets dancing along with more familiar blooms in his 'Ditty in Praise of Eliza, Queen of Shepherds':

> Bring hether the Pincke and purple Cullambine,
>> With Gelliflowres;
> Bring Coronations, and Sops-in-wine
>> Worne of Paramoures:
> Strowe me the ground with Daffadowndillies,
> And Cowslips, and Kingcups, and lovèd Lillies:
>> The pretie Pawnce,
>> And the Chevisaunce,
> Shall match with the fayre flowre Delice.

'Flowre Delice', presumably pronounced dillice, is Shakespeare's flower-de-luce, better known to us as fleur-de-lis, the heraldic lily or iris. Pawnce seems, like chevisance, to have withered away. Chevisance originally meant achievement or provision of supply and then, most unromantically, the lending of money or goods for profit. Spenser seems to have confused chevisance with chivalry: it is certainly too gentle a word for the usurers' profession, and is happier in the flower-bed than the counting-house.

CIT

A LEARNED essay might be written on the Abbreviation Contemptuous. Who calls a Gentleman a Gent is sneering: who reduces citizen to cit is doing much the same. But, after all, sneering is a part of wit and to reduce the swollen is usually both medical and moral. Cit is an excellent dismissive term, suggesting something less than a man in stature and more in purse. The cit, as most eighteenth-century authors knew, was wont to grub money in a dark counting-house in his mean little way. Wrote Burns:

> A title, Dempster merits it;
> A garter gie to Willie Pitt;
> Gie wealth to some be-ledger'd cit,
>> In cent. per cent.,
> But gie me real, sterling wit,
>> And I'm content.

Moderns should return to Cit. It may also surprise some of them to learn from Ayrshire that real was, and should remain, a word of two syllables.

CLOUD

A common climatic word, but no longer commonly employed, in its old and beautiful usage, to mean hill. At the southern base of the Pennines, in Cheshire and Derbyshire, it still is so applied and there you may climb a Cloud. That sounds magical and lyrical, but, as a matter of fact, cloud is, in origin, the same as clod. First a clod of rock, then a clod of air . . . but, with a stroke of genius or by accident, those designating clods of air started to use the far more gracious form cloud. And what an exquisite word it is, almost creating poetry with no more said!

> Like far-off mountains turnéd into clouds

is not one of the best-known lines in a very well-known play of Shakespeare, but it is certainly one of the loveliest, being most simply descriptive as well as musically perfect. Demetrius, if you are curious, says it to Hermia. (*A Midsummer Night's Dream*, Act iv, sc. 1). It unites the two meanings of cloud and for me has an enduring suggestion of mist over Dovedale, where some of the fells are Clouds.

36

A COGGING fellow is an excellent description of a cheating, cozening creature and pokes his nasty head up in the orations of the eighteenth century. To cog originally was to cheat at dice by manipulating the fall. Later it was simply to play the deceiver. Falstaff, courting Mistress Ford, puts cogging among the arts of the precious and the foppish.

> Come, I cannot cog, and say thou art this and that, like a many of these lisping hawthorn-buds, that come like women in men's apparel, and smell like Bucklersbury in simple-time;

It is queer that the word should have dropped out. The Victorians preferred pettifogging, which has not exactly the same sense since it implies smallness as well as duplicity. We should return to the attack on 'cogging politicians' and 'cogging, cozening, slaves'.

COMELY

TO use Comely now would, perhaps, be slightly affected, at least in England. It springs more naturally and with less archaic suggestion on Scottish lips. In 'The Song of Solomon' the Biblical translators used it of rich physical beauty: later it acquired a flavour of sobriety and moral decorum, adding these to the implication of a sensuous beauty. Milton's 'civil-suited Morn' was not 'trick'd and frounced' but 'kerchieft in a comely cloud'. Shakespeare's

> He is a man, setting his fate aside,
> Of comely virtues

makes the word first cousin to the austere 'seemly'. But a love who is 'black but comely' need not be so strict and in Scotland the fair word appears often to have been more liberally used, even of pleasuring places. In Edinburgh in the eighteenth century there was a resort called Comely Gardens, full of raree-shows, the intended Vauxhall of its time and city. Meanwhile the four Carnegie Trusts

in Dunfermline have one of the loveliest addresses that I know —
Comely Park House — and there do they properly survey and
assist the arts and learning as well as the moral and physical welfare
of the nation.

COMFORT

THIS is one of the admirable words which have turned soft and it
needs to be re-stiffened to its proper shape and value. It is, by
origin, the giver of strength and valour. But the ubiquitous advertisement of 'All Modern Comforts' hints mainly at central heating
and other niceties of plumbing. 'Comforts for the troops' would
once have been allies and reserves: listen to Berners' Froissart, who
wrote of companies, 'on a wyng in good order, ready to confort
the prince's batayle'. Now such comforts are mainly chocolates,
cigarettes, and woollies. One is not depreciating the pleasures and
utility of these latter in wishing more substance and dignity for the
grand old word. This has become so dwarfed and so insipid that
the unlettered Christian of to-day may easily think of the Holy
Ghost, the Comforter, as a rather sickly source of sentimental consolation, a celestial crooner almost, instead of as an ally in the good
fight and bringer of mettle and resolve. Gerard, the herbalist,
used comfortable to imply a tonic and strengthening power. 'If
odours may work satisfaction, they are so soveraigne in plants and
so comfortable that no confection of the apothecaries can equall
their excellent vertue.' Our comfort, in short, needs conforting
in the way of Tudor English.

COMPENDIUM

COMING across this word in some impolite contemporary observations on Oliver Cromwell ('That Landskip of Iniquity, that Sink of
Sin, and that Compendium of Baseness'), I was reminded of a
Christmas long ago when I received 'a Compendium of Games',
i.e. a chest containing the material for every kind of table-sport.

What a majestically Roman phrase for a somewhat bizarre, but
most serviceable article! Compendium usually means an abridge-
ment or summary or short treatise (e.g. Compendium of Mathe-
matics), but in the toy-market it is a collection, an Omnibus
Volume, as the publishers would say with an equal devotion to
Latin. It was an astonishingly august word to apply to a box of
childish pleasures and properly belonged to a seigneurial world in
which the channel of communication between drawing-room
and nursery was the imported polyglot governess. 'With what,
Fräulein, is Master Rupert engaged?' 'He is engaged, my lady, with
his Compendium.'

CORDIAL

As a noun it is commonly used for any warming drink, but more
rarely and effectively as any kind of life-sweetening and encouraging
thing. So it comes to mean an inspiriting example, as one might
describe a great comedian as 'the cordial of our stage'. Here it is in
John Galt, used in his description of Nanse Banks, who did the
village schooling for scholars' pence.

> She was a patient creature, well cut out for her calling, with
> blear een, a pale face, and a long neck, but meek and contented
> withal, tholing the dule of this word with a Christian sub-
> mission to the spirit; and her garret-room was a cordial of
> cleanliness.

Dule is exclusively Scots, but thole is good Anglo-classical for
endure. Cordial thus employed is 'a cordial of speech'.

COURTESY

I prefer courtesy to be pronounced not as the longer version of
curtsey but in the Victorian manner, with the 'ou' somewhat
Frenchified, as befits our cousin of the lovely 'courtoisie'. It means
the habit of being gracefully considerate in personal relations. It is

more than politeness; beauty breaks in. Chaucer set it beside truth, honour, and freedom. Belloc has an exquisite lyric on three pictures owned by the Storrington monks — 'and Courtesy was in them all'. He ends:

> Our Lady out of Nazareth rode —
> It was Her month of heavy load;
> Yet was Her face both great and kind,
> For Courtesy was in Her Mind.
>
> The Third it was our Little Lord,
> Whom all the Kings in arms adored;
> He was so small you could not see
> His large intent of Courtesy.

So fair a word deserves to be spoken finely and kept in honourable use.

CREATURE

CREATURES are of two kinds, those fashioned by Nature, which may be noble or base, well or ill-favoured, and those made by man, which are usually contemptible. This second use of creature may now savour of the antique, but it has sting in it. Looking recently at a programme of Shakespeare's *Richard II* I noticed Bushy, Bagot, and Green described as 'Creatures of King Richard', which is far better than the 'servants to King Richard' usually employed. Let us have our more servile Members of Parliament dismissed as Creatures, instead of Puppets, of the Party Whips. There is something, at least for me, luridly 'umble, creepy, and crawly about a creature of this kind. Shakespeare, by the way, deprives the king's creatures of their proper titles. Holinshed wrote:

The common brute ran that the king had set to farme the realme of England unto Sir William Scroope, Earl of Wiltshire, and then treasurer of England, to Sir John Bushie, Sir William Bagot, and Sir Henry Greene, knights.

The common brute is good: it so bluntly forecasts for us one phase of the modern industry of information.

CRIMSON

WHEN I first read, in a fine Scots ballad,

> When we cam in by Glasgow toun,
>   We were a comely sicht to see:
> My love was clad in the black velvet
>   And I myself in cramasie,

I would have answered any question about the nature of cramasie by saying that it was a species of gay cloth named after some foreign place, as cretonne is named after Creton in Normandy. But cramasie is the old Scots form of crimson, itself a comely word, but no aboriginal, however native it may sound. It is, in fact, a Middle-Eastern import and one of our many Arabians. It is also, like other arrivals from the gorgeous east, an insect. Cramasie and cremosin, later crimson, came from the Arabic Qerinasi, the cochineal insect which, on being crushed in quantity, yields a reddish-purple dye. Out of this sordid mush comes our rich and romantic name of crimson, a name which always reminds me of one of the most strangely beautiful Shakespearean passages. When Iachimo is standing over the sleeping Imogen he spies,

>   On her left breast
>   A mole cinque-spotted, like the crimson drops
>   I' the bottom of a cowslip.

The next time you pick a cowslip, look within, not only to appreciate the imperial mixture of crimson and yellow, but the exquisite sharpness of Shakespeare's eye that went to the making of this simile.

CRINKUM-CRANKUM

HERE is a fine dismissive word for all the fussily over-decorated things. Lord Ogleby in Coleman's comedy, *The Clandestine Marriage*, thus dismissed the vogue of Gothic which, in the middle of the eighteenth century, was beginning to fill the grounds of an English Nobleman's Seat with sham ruins and twisty ponds. At that time canals, not yet industrialized, were still channels (the words are really the same) and the gardens of a great mansion had to be rich in such ornamental waters. Fashion continually made the canals more bizarre, equipped them with a false façade of bogus bridges, and even introduced the fantastic Italian style of grotto with curious fountains, vivarium, aquarium, and so forth. All, of course, to be designed 'with knobs on', as the modern slang so expressively describes a certain kind of architecture. In short, crinkum-crankum.

DAEDAL

DAEDAL is pure classicism, deriving from Daedalus, the inventive one, and used both of the contriving hand and of the multiplicity of things contrived, especially by Nature. *Natura naturans* is daedal in one sense, *Natura naturata* in the other. Evelyn, the Diarist, wrote of 'a Daedale' as a complicated device in the laying out of gardens. Landor liked the word with its suggestion of multitudinous and glittering growth or movement. To him a dance was daedal. Robert Louis Stevenson implied a gloriously daedal world in his famous

> God's bright and intricate device
> Of days and seasons.

To Lord de Tabley, that gifted as well as baronial bard, looking out over Tabley Mere in Cheshire, a county which long remained lordly in a quiet way, the month of May and the pinguid scene ('Earth's royal aspects of delight') suggested the classic epithet. He saw

The serene domes of mounting lime
The meadow's crest of daedal May
And deep-eyed morning ere the time,
Sleeking her curtain clouds away.

I am indebted to Sir William Beach Thomas and his rustic anthology
'The Squirrels' Granary' for being reminded of de Tabley's
excellence.

DAFF

THERE are two Daffs, apart from the abbreviation of Daffodil.
There is the Scottish Daff, which is to talk or behave sportively. In
Jane Elliot's *The Flowers of the Forest* when 'The English, for ance,
by guile won the day', the melancholy has reached the sheep-folds
and there is sad silence at the milking-pails.

Lasses are lonely and dowie and wae
Nae daffin', nae gabbin' . . .

A dowie, i.e. dismal, lass may be the opposite of a daffin' one in
meaning, but she is equal in felicity of phrase. The English Daff
is to put off, cast aside. Clothes are both daffed and doffed. Daffing
may be applied to far larger matters than a doublet. 'Canst thou so
daff me?' cries Leonato when Claudio is pushing him away.
Henry V was once the Mad-Cap Prince who 'daffed the world
aside'. Why did his posterity daff this trim, expressive term?

DAFFODIL

DAFF I have claimed to be twice virtuous, once on each side of
the Tweed. But it becomes abominable when used as an abbreviation of Daffodil, a word so fair that truncation is a vile malpractice.
Daffodil itself is a childish creation (daffadowndilly still more so)
and a nursery version, as it were, of Affodil, which, in turn, is our
conception of Asphodel. Poetry is forever candled with the light

of Asphodel, as Elysium was carpeted with its blooms. When I was introduced to Asphodel on the Greek mountains beside Mycenae, I was as much disappointed by the first as staggered by the majesty of the second. Presumably I was shown the wrong article, for it bore no resemblance to our 'lamp of beauty', Shakespeare's brave anticipator of the swallow. Asphodel shall remain for me a lyric love, a flower laid up in fancy, frequent in the grounds of Castle Bunthorne — as well as in the classic meadows. English lyric poetry sways and shines with the windswept gold of daffodils. They are summoned to a lamentation by Milton.

> Bid amaranthus all his beauty shed
> And daffadillies fill their cups with tears,
> To strew the laureate hearse where Lycid lies.

But for the most part they are vessels of rejoicing.

DAINTY

ANOTHER of the victims of softening. It comes from the old French version of dignity and means anything of merit, value, and esteem. It grew to include fastidiousness and then, for some reason, it was depressed to the signification of the softly pretty and quaint. 'Teas', for example, as served in Ye Olde Oake Tea Roomes or the God-Wottery Gardens of the Kozy Kafe, are inevitably 'dainty'. Dainty, indeed, in modern English, has become almost exclusively applied to this blend of 'arty' china and horrid little cakes, just as 'prime' has now become attached exclusively to the leading Minister of State and the better cuts of butcher's meat. An Elizabethan could have asked for a dainty steak and expected a fine, big one. Such an order to-day, if understood at all, would produce a mouthful, probably minced. 'Full many a deynte hors hadde he in stable' is the real Old English, and not 'Ye Olde' at all. John Fletcher linked dainty with the lusty spring, and he too wrote,

Green woods are dumb,
And will never tell to any
Those dear kisses and those many
Sweet embraces that are given:
Dainty pleasures that would even
Raise in coldest age a fire,
And give virgin-blood desire.

The pleasures here are evidently vigorous.

When Prospero says 'That's my dainty Ariel' he is thanking the spirit for his aid, not commenting on ethereal fragility. The 'dainty dish' of old was a dish worth eating, not a pretty fragment.

DAMASK

THE Syrian city of Damascus has, through its crafts, added picturesquely to our lexicon. A sword, a silk, a linen, a rose, all these have at some time, and even at the same time, been damask. Because linen is bleached and blanched, damask suggests whiteness to some. It may have done so to Bacon when he wrote 'roses, damask and red are fast flowers of their smell, so that you may walk in a whole row of them and find nothing of their sweetness'. But the true damask rose, of which attar of roses was made, was a pink flower and so the lips and complexions of Tudor ladies were frequently damask to the poet. Who can forget Viola's,

She never told her love
But let concealment, like a worm i' the bud,
Feed on her damask cheek?

The verb, to damascene, means to ornament with inlaid work or watered pattern. John Davidson, too little remembered, often combined the rich vocabulary of late nineteenth-century 'poetese' with his relentless reasonings. His

arabesques of blue and emerald wave
Begin to damascene the iron sea

45

dexterously links in its metaphors the Syrian city with the Arabian deserts adjoining. His was a period of damascened English, with Oscar Wilde, in his flowery phases, as first practitioner.

DANDER

DANDER has a strange assortment of meanings. It can be a cinder or a piece of scurf or a show of temper. But it is also, and far better, a wandering or stroll. The Scots have retained this usage, and wisely — for what more expressive of an easy walk at dusk than 'a wee bit dander in the gloaming'? The very slowness of the movement is in the word. The English have preferred saunter, which is also happily expressive. But I always have the sense of the right noise for a slow and pleasant vagabondage when I read in a Scots book of a dander in the glen. The Mearns on a summer night, the Mearns so richly and rhythmically described in Lewis Grassic Gibbon's tremendous novels of the eastern Scottish coast and its dwindling crofter life, *Sunset Song* and *Cloud Howe*, is rare dandering country, as it ripples between the Grampians and the sea. When you read of such crofts and villages as Kinraddie and Blawaerie and Peesies' Knapp and of the peewits and curlews above them, it's a dander that any wise man would be having in 'the lithe' of the hills, as Gibbon would say, lithe here meaning cover or recess.

DAPPER

DAPPER nowadays suggests a gentleman with patent-leather hair, well-creased trousers, and spats (if it be a good spat year). But Milton was not thinking of the best-dressed fairy when he wrote,

> The Sounds and Seas with all their finny drove
> Now to the Moon in wavering Morrice move,
> And on the Tawny Sands and Shelves
> Trip the pert Fairies and the dapper Elves;

46

Dapper to him meant quick and alert. Johnson defined it 'Little and active, lively without bulk'. Elves could not have an apter epithet. It is a pity that so vital a word has been annexed by haberdashery.

DAZE

IT is right that the North should have the best terms for cold. The South has lost the use of daze for numb, narrowing its usage to strong effects on eye and brain, just as it has limited 'starve' to matters of appetite. The Yorkshire child who, when settled in an air-raid shelter of the dank and draughty kind, cried out to his mother, 'Ee Moom, ba goom, ma boom is noom' might have called his posterior dazed had he lived a little earlier. In Scotland the use of daze does, I believe, linger. How well it sits in Gavin Douglas's sharp, clear, and tingling description of a Scottish winter.

> In this congealit season sharp and chill,
> The caller air penetrative and pure,
> Dazing the blude in every creature,
> Made seek warm stovis and bene fyris hot.
> In double garment cled and wyliecoat,
> With michty drink, and meatis confortive . . .

The last robust and reassuring word surely amplifies and justifies my earlier note on the original implication of comfort.

DEBAUCHEE

WORDS ending in -ee frequently give pleasure. Debauch is both expressive in sound and curious in origin. It comes from an old French word meaning 'to turn away from the workshop' and thus lead into idleness. The familiar connotation of idleness with sin followed and debauchery meant indulgence in the sensual joys. (This must remind many an old Oxonian, who followed philosophy under Canon Rashdall, of that rubicund divine's nice division of happiness into (a) Religious Rapture and (b) Violent, Sensual Pleasure.) Debauchee was a term which I loved to use when young in translating the observations of Cicero and Demosthenes on their opponents. I met it with delight recently in a series of anonymous eighteenth century 'Letters from Edinburgh', in which an English visitor described Scottish habits. He very strangely regarded the reel as a dance 'trifling and insipid'. Yet this trifle could evoke a thirst in at least its masculine practitioners, which disgusted the English looker-on. The Scottish gentry, he said, after the ladies are withdrawn,

> retire into a private room, where each sacrifices his under-standing and health to wining, in full bumpers, the health of his fair partner; who, if she has any understanding, must ridicule, condemn, and abhor the custom. But the Scotch Gentlemen are so resolute in their determination, that many of them, immediately after the departure of the Ladies, retire for a short time, in order to change their dancing apparel, and put on a dress more adapted to the occasion of riot and excess.

Strange goings-on! Small wonder that the horrified Englishman wrote of his hosts as 'debauchees'.

DESCANT

MOST of our musical terms begin with a strict technical reference and then are applied, with a sentimental enthusiasm, to melody in general. (See later note on Madrigal.) Descant stood for the earliest form of counterpoint, but the Elizabethan poets, all of them musicians and primed with the lore and language of the art, seized it for song and harmony in general, and also made a verb of it. So, too, diapason, the concord through all the notes of the scale, comes to be used for all far-ranging agreement. Neither is a particularly attractive word, but the Elizabethans had a cunning and delightful knack of working the vocabulary of the music master into the music of the heart and Drayton, proclaiming the sad sighs of passion, cunningly employed such terms as these:

> My hollow sighs the deepest base do beare
> True diapazon in distincted sound:
> My panting hart the treble makes the ayre,
> And descants finely on the musique's ground;
> Thus like a Lute or Viol did I lye,
> Whilst he, proud slave, daunced galliards in her eye.

Descant was also used as a verb to mean simply talk or comment. Shakespeare has it both ways. Julia in *Two Gentlemen of Verona* is said to 'mar the concord with too harsh a descant', while Richard Crookback would 'descant' on his own deformity.

DIM

SHORT, simple dim, source of emotion in many a moving line, has had radically different meanings. To Shakespeare it mainly conveyed the idea of darkness. Tombs are dim, cloudy skies are dim, and 'violets dim' (magical phrase, as only Shakespeare could make magic of the simplest words) must refer to darkness of hue. Yet the notion of faintness was also implicit in his use of the word at times. 'As dim and meagre as an ague's fit', he says of a dying child. Milton's 'dim, religious light' perhaps unites both conceptions. Later the idea of something vague, weak, and transient begins to supplant the concept of darkness. In my undergraduate days dim, in our cant, stood for anything grey or dull. A witless or uninteresting man was voted dim. Dim in the sense of evanescent or ghostly occurs with magnificence in Siegfried Sassoon's sonnet 'On Passing the New Menin Gate'.

> Crudely renewed the Salient holds its own,
> Paid are its dim defenders by that pomp:
> Paid, with a pile of peace-complacent stone,
> The armies who endured that sullen swamp.

Browning finely alliterated it in his famous

> Still one must lead some life beyond,
> Have a bliss to die with, dim-descried.

Dim is but a meek, mild, midget of a word, but it has contributed to gigantic utterance, of which I take these to be examples.

DISASTER

A COMMON word and one which has lost its heavenly significance. The 'aster' is the Greek and Latin word for 'star' and so disaster is the ill-starred thing. To the writers of the sixteenth and seventeenth centuries it still had that significance of destiny proclaimed by the motions of the heavenly bodies. Edmund in *King Lear* links it with the skies.

> when we are sick in fortune, — often the surfeit of our own behaviour, — we make guilty of our disasters the sun, the moon, and the stars: as if we were villains by necessity; fools by heavenly compulsion: knaves, thieves, and treachers by spherical predominance; drunkards, liars, and adulterers by an enforced obedience of planetary influence; and all that we are evil in, by a divine thrusting on:'

Horatio in *Hamlet* reminds us how,

> A little ere the mightiest Julius fell,
> The graves stood tenantless, and the sheeted dead
> Did squeak and gibber in the Roman streets:
> As, stars with trains of fire and dews of blood,
> Disasters in the sun; and the moist star,
> Upon whose influence Neptune's empire stands,
> Was sick almost to doomsday with eclipse:

'Disasters in the sun' is a most curious phrase. The sky still enfolds the word, but the exact and starry meaning has vanished. In our time disaster has been unskied and belittled altogether. It used to be seen in Italy over Goods for Sale. Where we write 'Bankrupt Stock, Forced Sale', the Italians were apt to announce simply 'Disastro'. It has the ring of doom.

DISTASTE

NOT an impressive verb, perhaps, but it must be the peg for a note on Shakespeare's delight in the prefix dis-, which he often used where un- would be normal (e.g. dispiteous for unpitiful and disnatured for unnatural). Distasted means spoilt or put out of flavour and occurs in one of the least known among the loveliest of passages in Shakespeare. When Troilus and Cressida must part, Troilus cries,

> We two, that with so many thousand sighs
> Did buy each other, must poorly sell ourselves
> With the rude brevity and discharge of one.
> Injurious time now, with a robber's haste,
> Crams his rich thievery up, he knows not how:
> As many farewells as be stars in heaven,
> With distinct breath and consign'd kisses to them,
> He fumbles up into a loose adieu;
> And scants us with a single famish kiss,
> Distasted with the salt of broken tears.

There is the very agony of war-time parting forever pictured, with poignancy unmatchable, the short, snatched kiss of the railway-platform or the quay-side as the train goes out or the ship sails. If anybody is interested in Shakespeare's exquisite and no doubt unconscious use of alliteration, let him note the use of 's', letter of sighs, in the last five lines; the 's' is most delicately interlaced with the many 'l's, three initial 'f's, two 'd's, two 'k's, and the plentiful 't's of the last line. To me the last couplet is as moving as anything that Shakespeare ever wrote and very nearly brings that physical shiver down the spine which A. E. Housman took to be the circumstance and proof of mighty poetry.

DOWIE

DOES dowie linger anywhere in northern English dialect? It was good Scots (and should stay so) for all things dull and heavy. Wrote Skinner, the author of *Tullochgorum*, of what he deemed to be 'dull, Italian lays':

> They're dowf and dowie at the best
> Their allegros and a' the rest,
> They canna please a Scottish taste
> Compared wi' Tullochgorum.

(Dowf is a word of almost similar meaning.) Skinner's vigorous salutation to the reel and contempt of Italian modes may show a less than subtle ear for fine music, but he knew fine words. Dowie is excellently used in Robert Fergusson's picture of the kind of winter morn when it is better to be 'canty' in the city of Edinburgh than 'cauldrife' on the farm. He knows and echoes his Skinner and bids the musicians

> Roset well your fiddle-sticks
> But banish vile Italian tricks
> Frae out your quorum,
> Nor fortes with pianos mix;
> Gie's Tullochgorum.

That is conventional Scots revel. What is not so ordinary and is indeed sharply descriptive is the first verse of this piece, 'The Daft Days'.

> Now mirk December's dowie face
> Glow's owr're the rigs wi' sour grimace
> While, through his minimum of space,
> The bleer-ee'd sun
> Wi' blinkin' light and stealin' pace
> His race doth run.

The first line has all mid-winter in its dank, tenebrous chill. Burns learned much from Fergusson, whose death at twenty-four, when the Ayrshire lad was fifteen, robbed Edinburgh of a master-singer.

DRAFFISH

DRAFFISH sounds like a telescoped form of dregs and raffish and that, in fact, does give its meaning. Draff, suggesting the lees or worthless residue, was a favourite of John Milton's, whose Samson asks only to drudge

> Till vermin or the draff of servil food
> Consume me.

The brood of Belial is also referred to as human 'draff'. Draffish, as an antiquity restored, would serve very well to describe not only the patrons of certain night-clubs, but the kind of food and drink which they are so eager to consume at preposterous prices.

DUDGEON

DUDGEON to Shakespeare was the wooden handle of a knife — 'And on thy blade and dudgeon gouts of blood', said Macbeth of his visionary dagger. Why did it come to mean peevishness and why is it now always high, though, in the seventeenth century, it could also be deep? I find no answer. Dudgen (without the 'o') is a now obsolete word for trash or trashy. Is our slang word dud an abbreviation of this or did it come from the notion that duds are ragged clothes? I had always believed that duds were the flashing clothes and haberdashery connected with dudes. Dude is set down as a recent American importation, but I suspect it of being reimported and possibly very old English.

DULCIFY

POLONIUS deemed beautify a vile word. Would he have been so sharply dismissive of the similar dulcify?

If we are ever to prefer the Latin to the Saxon term, surely we may sweeten sweetness by admitting dulcitude and dulcify, which make such a comfortable noise. 'Can you sublime and dulcify?' asks Subtle in *The Alchemist* of the astonished Ananias. Here, of course, the reference is chemical, but the words are most suitable for application to any fragment of man's business upon earth. Art, morals, politics — may we not hope to see them all, in their various ways, sublimed and dulcified? They make a handsome couple.

DUMPISH

THOUGH dumps and dumpishness sometimes refer to stupidity, they originally meant, as they do most commonly now, a dull form of melancholy.

> When griping grief the heart doth wound
> And doleful dumps the mind oppress.

How many Shakespeareans will place that quotation at a glance? (The source is *Romeo and Juliet*, Act iv. sc. 5, if you confess to ignorance and want the information. It is, however, a quotation from a poem 'In Commendation of Musick' by Richard Edwards.) One of the most captivating uses of the word is in the negative and as a verb. Here is Fuller on the great clown Tarlton, the Grimaldi of Tudor England. 'Our Tarlton was master of his Faculty. When Queen Elizabeth was serious (I dare not say sullen) and out of good humour, he could undumpish her at his pleasure.' Fortunate Tarlton, whose targets for to-night did not have to include professional dramatic critics, who creep like snails unwillingly to stall. True, they in the end give the droll his immortality, but they can be a terrible affliction in the meantime to those who would live by undumpishing. A Dump was a technical Elizabethan term for a lament. John Davies of Hereford wrote 'A Dump upon the death of the most noble Henrie, late Earle of Pembrooke.'

ENERGUMEN

To my astonishment I came across energumen in my morning paper and, though its general meaning was apparent, I had to consult the dictionary for the history and precise implication of this ugly but energetic word. It is a direct transliteration from the Greek. An energumen is not somebody ferociously working, but a person ferociously worked upon, chiefly by a devil or a frenzy. So an energumen is a demoniac enthusiast and raving devotee. The word, which was first employed in the beginning of the eighteenth century, may be rare, but the odious creature whom it depicts has been appallingly common in twentieth century Europe.

ESSENTIAL

This is a word which has been twisted away from its proper meaning. It should imply an article with essence, that is with genuine quality in it, and so substantial, important, full, pregnant. Now, of course, it is merely a synonym for necessary. It would be nice to hear again of an essential picture or poem. Milton magnificently gives us the negative side of the word.

> The void profound
> Of unessential Night receives him next
> Wide gaping, and with utter loss of being
> Threatens him plunged in that abortive gulf.

These lines most powerfully suggest to me the spectacle of my colleague in dramatic criticism, Mr. James Agate, sitting, under compulsion, at a musical comedy.

FANCY

Few words have so sadly come down in the world as fancy. It began (in its full form of phantasy) as the supreme quality of imagination. It is now an epithet for sugared or bedizened things, fancy bread (Scottish for cakes and biscuits) or fancy work, which implies any kind of irrelevant and hideous decoration. Fancy cooking is the 'good, plain cook's' dismissal of anything ambitious on the menu. Members of the fancy, now abbreviated to 'fans', may once have been connoisseurs of a sport, even of an art. (De Quincey used it of the bookish.) Now they are gaping, doltish creatures who make divinities of film-stars and scramble for autographs. That is the final degradation of fancy, which to Shakespeare meant the flight of mind and surge of feeling, the source of passion and of poetry too. To his Cleopatra fancy is the highest form of imagination. When asked if there might be another such as Antony she replies that Nature, in making such a man, defied all fancy, 'condemning shadows quite'. To Orsino, most musical of lovers, fancy is an honoured name for love itself.

FANGLE

FANGLE for a fashion has almost disappeared, surviving only in the adjective new-fangled and, less commonly, in the opposite, old-fangled. Shakespeare has the adjective fangled, Porthumus talking of 'our fangled world' in which the epithet has passed on from the meaning of affectation to that of deceitfulness. The dwindling use of fangle, except in a compound, reminds one of other useful words which have vanished, except in some negative or comparative form. The Scots have held to couth or couthy for kind, gentle, or cosy. ('Couthy and bien' — to rhyme with green — sang Stevenson of the sheltered house 'atween the muckle Pentland's knees'.) The English have let it go (absurdly, for 'a couthy farm' is a beautiful description of a steading lying snug in rich land) and retained the negative form, uncouth, applying it specially to roughness of aspect and manners. But if the lads of the village are to be uncouth, may not the lasses of the town be couth or couthy?

FAREWELL

THE word has dropped out of popular speech. We say 'Good-bye', which is decent, or decline into the democratic 'ta-ta's' and 'cheerios' and 'so longs', which are miserable. (What exactly does 'So long' mean?) Farewell is now rather literary or slightly jocose. Perhaps this is due to a kind of reverence. Do we hesitate to make common a word which sounds so beautiful? You have only to put it in a line that scans and poetry emerges.

> Farewell the tranquil mind: farewell content!
> Farewell the plumed troop and the big wars
> That make ambition virtue! O farewell!
> Farewell the mighty steed and the shrill trump
> The spirit-stirring drum, the ear-piercing fife,
> The royal banner and all quality
> Pride, pomp, and circumstance of glorious war
> . . .
> Farewell, Othello's occupation's gone.

Substitute good-bye for farewell in these lines, and the magic entirely vanishes. The word has the rich melancholy of Rome's 'Ave atque Vale', which must be pronounced with the 'a' broad. One of the loneliest sheep-farms in the noble wilderness of the North Yorkshire moors is called 'Farewell'. The people who so named it had the unconscious genius of the ballad-maker.

FASCINATE

MOST words descend in value: fascinate has actually climbed in reputation. It now refers mainly to attractive and radiantly enchanting things. To call a woman fascinating would be wholly complimentary. But once it would have been an accusation of witchcraft and even a stake-and-faggot matter. Fascinate originally meant to submit to the evil eye and exact writers, like W. H. Hudson, would still so apply it. He used it, for example, of the uncanny spell exercised on other animals and on small birds by the stoat and weasel. Either of these can paralyse the former, denying them power of motion, and leaving them staggering and screaming in terror, the latter they allure to come ever lower down the twigs, twittering in morbid ecstasy, until they are within striking distance of the fierce, blood-lusty fangs. In Hudson's *Hampshire Days* there is a wonderful picture of this fascination in progress in a wood near Boldre, where he watched a weasel chattering and spinning madly round the base of a tree, while an audience of birds, 'chaffinches, wrens, robins, dunnocks, ox-eyes, willow-wrens, and chiff-chaffs', fluttered spell-bound ever closer to the crazy cunning of their foe. After such fascination (Hudson calls it 'the good, old word') one might be inclined to avoid it in social compliment, but the ancient connection with the evil eye has been entirely forgotten. So let the greenwood tree, as well as the lady fair, be our fascinator now.

FEAT AND FEATEOUS

To Shakespeare feat was an adjective as well as a noun. We have lost the adjective both in its brief form of feat and its longer one of feateous. Imogen became 'a page so feat, so nurse-like' and Perdita danced so 'featly' as to win the perfect tribute

> When you dance, I wish you
> A wave o' the sea, that you might ever do
> Nothing but that.

Feat as an adjective means neat, trim, efficient, and feateous (sometimes featous) also means well-shaped and becoming. The water nymphs of Thames in Spenser's stately 'Prothalamion' were feateous in their plucking of the bridal bouquets.

> And each one had a little wicker basket
> Made of fine twigs, entrailéd curiously,
> In which they gathered flowers to fill their flasket,
> And with fine fingers cropt full feateously
> The tender stalks on high.

Feateous would be a happy term for all actions in which skill and beauty run in beauty together. Games should have their feateous players as well as their feats and records. Prince Obolensky, who was killed in an air-crash early in the war, was feateous indeed upon the Rugby Football field. He touched some games that he could not win, none that he did not decorate.

FLOOSIE

SUCH terms as 'blowen', already mentioned, and 'frisgig' and 'giglot', yet to have their note, may be thought to cover sufficiently the frailty of women. But the American 'floosie' is so picturesque as to deserve a recognition. It may be Old English. You never know with American slang. So let us accept it as a novelty. It has a blousy, flowery atmosphere and, to me, at least, immediately and richly suggests a substantial charmer with plenty of good spirits and bad scent.

FOISON

OUR words for abundance do not abound and it seems regrettable that foison should be only an antiquity. It comes from the Latin for pouring and signifies the effusion of the horn of plenty. Perhaps its decay is due to an unhappy similarity to poison. Whatever the reason, we could do with it to help the painting of our summer landscape. I am writing this looking out on to English fields upon a 'glorious first of June' and what words have we to suggest the astonishing tangle and strength, the jungle-richness of early summer's growth in a soft and fruitful shire? Six weeks ago there was scarcely a sign of all this (it was a very tardy spring) and now we have Lucio's 'teeming foison', Gonzalo's 'all foison, all abundance', and the 'Earth's increase and foison plenty' sung by Ceres. There is general foison of crop and weed, of serviceable copse and ruinous briar. Perhaps another and more closely Latin word will help one to describe the lushness of the meadows and hedges. That is 'pinguid', a vivid word for fat pastures, but another Elizabethan casualty. 'From death to life thou might'st him yet recover', as Drayton sang of another matter.

FOXED

I T is strange that foxy should mean cunning while foxed means baffled and stupid. In the latter sense it now has a Victorian ring. Only gentlemen of the oldest school would talk about being 'properly foxed' by liquor or calamity. It was a favourite of Pepys. After the Coronation of Charles II Pepys sat late with the Yeoman of the Royal Wine-cellar.

> With his wife and two of his sisters, and some gallant sparks that were there, we drank the King's health, and nothing else, till one of the gentlemen fell down stark drunk, and there lay, and I went to my lord's pretty well. But no sooner abed with Mr. Shepley, but my head began to turn, and I to vomit, and if ever I was foxed, it was now.

Later on,

> Waked in the morning with my head in a sad taking through the last night's drink, which I am very sorry for: so rose, and went out with Mr. Creed to drink our morning draught, which he did give me in chocolate to settle my stomach.

Chocolate, as antidote to a hang-over, would leave some of us queasy moderns more 'foxed' than ever.

FRIBBLE

T o fribble is to act feebly, to be frivolous in a petty, fiddling way. The verb is also used as a noun, a fribble being a trifler. Its close rhyme with dribble suggests to me a dotard far-gone in years and folly. Mr. Justice Shallow was the fribble at his most likeable. Captain Charles Morris, who wrote some genial, toss-pot rhymes in the eighteenth century, observes:

> I find too when I stint my glass
> > And sit with sober air,
> I'm prosed by some dull, reasoning ass
> > Who treads the path of care;

> Or, harder tax'd, I'm forced to bear
>   Some coxcomb's fribbling strain,
> And that I think's a reason fair
>   To fill my glass again.

To be prosed, as a passive verb, is good and should appeal to all who have been much pent in conventicles and lecture-rooms.

FRISGIG

THIS, for a silly young woman, is not an orthodox dictionary word, but well it might be, for it is an excellent example of the vividness of Lancashire dialect. It so nicely telescopes the friskiness and giggles of a lively, vapid miss that it really ought to be taken into common English usage. It reminds me of the Elizabethan giglot, which began by meaning a wanton and then, because of its closeness in sound to giggle, went on to suggest a party both more innocent and more infuriating, the tittering, romping wench. Giglot, as well as frisgig, merits renewal, especially in its later sense. For wantons we had, and have, so many words. Ben Jonson alone will yield a column or so, of which callet is the chilliest and fricatrice the most candid. There are fewer terms for the titterers. So what Lancashire thought on this subject yesterday, England might well think again to-morrow.

FROLIC

FROLIC is almost always a noun or a verb to us, as it was to Thomas Woodcock who wrote of academic life and its oddities in the later seventeenth century,

> Of Dr. Thomas Goodwin, when ffelow of Catharine Hall. —
> He was somewhat whimsycall, in a frolick pist once in old
> Mr. Lothian's pocket (this I suppose was before his trouble of
> conscience and conversion made him serious). . . . He prayed
> with his hatt on and sitting.

It is perhaps as well that the donnish sense of a frolic has since altered. But it is a pity that the same century's use of frolic as an adjective has virtually disappeared. Milton's 'frolic wind that breathes the spring' is, of course, familiar. Herrick found wine to be both 'frolick' and 'frantick'. 'Come shake the frolic cocktail on the ice' would ring well to-day. There are occasions, no doubt, when frantic would be more accurately applied to that form of refreshment.

FRUITION

FRUITION, rightly used, is a delightful word. But how often is it so employed? Even the most august authors may be daily discovered confusing it with fruit and maturity. Leader-writers continually hold forth about plans 'coming to fruition'. The word, in fact, has nothing to do with fruit, but is derived from the Latin 'fruor', I enjoy, and means enjoyment. The meaning of ripeness, says the O.E.D. firmly, 'is not countenanced by dictionaries in this country, nor by Webster'. Fruition was rightly and exquisitely used by Marlowe.

> That perfect bliss and sole felicity,
> The sweet fruition of an earthly crown.

Charles Lamb in his rhymed 'Farewell to Tobacco' moaned, correctly as well as pathetically, that he had lost his seat among the 'blest Tobacco Boys'.

> Where, though I, by sour physician,
> Am debarr'd the full fruition
> Of thy favours, I may catch
> Some collateral sweets, and snatch
> Sidelong odours, that give life
> Like glances from a neighbour's wife;

We owe it to Marlowe and to Lamb to save fruition from the hackneyed misuse to which modern ignorance and carelessness have brought it.

GALINGALE

GOING back to boyhood's favourites, some of the more golden reaches of Tennysonian iambic (Why not? I find them delightfully rich in lullaby quality and excellent for perusal during air-raids), I ran into galingale. For Tennyson it decorated the land of the Lotus-eaters.

> Border'd with palm and many a winding vale,
> And meadow, set with slender galingale.

The galingale, which to us may suggest some 'period' boskage among which a lady in a farthingale listened to a nightingale, is an Eastern aromatic root. The Elizabethan men, so avid of all spices, used it carnally for cooking, but Tennyson, more loftily, for atmosphere. Remaking its acquaintance led to some dictionary-loitering in which I was reminded of the jovial and fine-sounding mixture of words beginning with 'gal'. Here is a question for a General Knowledge Paper. Distinguish between, Galingale, Galipot, Galligaskin, Gallimaufry, and Gallowglass. Also between Galliard and Galliass.

GALLIMAUFRY

ONE answer, at least, shall be given to the previous queries.

A good-sounding medley or hodge-podge is gallimaufry and one that came easily to the roaring play-boys and pamphleteers of Tudor London. Nashe, commenting on the stage of his time ('Our players are not as the players beyond sea, a sort of squirting bawdy comedians') goes on to complain that the ancient Romans always over-praised and over-wrote their native talent, 'thinking scorn to any but domestic examples of their own home-bred actors, scholars, and champions: and them they would extol to the third and fourth generation: cobblers, tinkers, fencers, none escaped them, but they mingled their all in one gallimaufry of glory'.

This last attractively alliterative phrase itself sums up the temper and achievements of Nashe's aspiring, brilliant, and cantankerous world, a gallimaufry of fiery particles. Incidentally, was ever a tedious stream of third-rate smut so brilliantly punished in a phrase as by 'a sort of squirting, bawdy comedians'?

GENIAL

WHAT an odd multiplicity of meanings has genial! 'Of or pertaining to the chin', for example. So a man may talk of 'a genial shave' or, with double truth, of Mr. Jack Hulbert as a most 'genial comedian'. But that is a different genial altogether from the commoner word, which, in its turn, has abundant variety of usage. 'Of or pertaining to marriage, nuptial.' 'Of or pertaining to a feast, festive.' So to our sympathetic, encouraging, jovial forms of geniality. Milton, loyal as ever to the original implication, spoke of the spirit presiding over marriage and fertility as 'The Genial Angel' and Spenser's description of matrimony as genial refers to the function as well as to the fun. Now good spirits have entirely usurped the term. There is a most solemn use of it in Collins's *Ode to Evening*, where he curiously links it with 'The pensive pleasures' brought by evening's 'genial lov'd return'.

GLAMOUR

THIS beautiful word has been bludgeoned to death by modern showmanship, which has attached it to every young lady who contributes a face to the film or a limb to the chorus. It is an English importation from Scotland where it had long signified magic with magical effect. I had fancied that it was pronounced 'glam-oor' until I found Burns rhyming it with grammar.

> Ye gipsy gangs that deal in glamour
> And you deep read in hell's black grammar.

Until quite recently glamour was reserved for conjuring tricks and was not bestowed, as now with such damnable iteration, on all aspiring to or professing 'it', 'umph' or 'sex-appeal', to use the modish titles of what used to be called plain loveliness. It was really Mr. David Devant who had true glamour in my boyhood, not Miss Gabrielle Ray. Jugglers and magicians were said to cast glamour, as it were dust, over the eyes of the public and even Tennyson used the word of wizardry. (It is noticeable that the word 'wizard' was recently a smart-slang term for anything attractive or excellent.) Now glamour and glamorous are tagged on, with infuriating frequency, to any kind of tinsel pleasure or personality. Chorus Girls, so dear to the Edwardians, have ceased to exist. They are all Glamour Girls now.

GLAUCOUS

THIS is simply a transliteration from the Greek and Latin and, as a rule, so close a classicism makes poor English. But here, surely, is an exception. Have we any single word which so well describes the usual tint of our national border and bulwark? 'Of a full green colour passing into greyish blue', says the O. E. D. Not the sea at its radiant best or white with anger, but in its normal hue. Day after day our shores are set about with glaucosity and no other word so comprehensively establishes the hue of our firths and channels in an average view. Cries Shelley's Panthea,

> 'Ere-while I slept
> Under the glaucous caverns of old Ocean,

Often enough we have tried to sleep on top of them. To spend a week or more gazing at the glaucous wilderness can be very boring, and perhaps glaucous, with its ponderous surge of sound, does also suggest the heavy hours and heaving motion of a voyage prolonged.

GLEEK

WHY has gleek for jest, both verb and noun, so largely disappeared? It is curt and expressive. 'I have seen you gleeking and galling at

E   65

the gentleman,' says Gower to Pistol, with reference to Fluellen. There is some punning point there because the episode includes the compulsion to eat a leek. But Shakespeare also used the word straightforwardly. 'I can gleek upon occasion', said Bottom to Titania. We might follow his example.

GRACE

How lucky our Dukes have been to inherit a title of such high privilege, for grace has long been blessed among English words, signifying beauty both of body and of matter. The divine Graces of the pagans were the bestowers of all forms of loveliness and of 'a laughing way in the teeth of the world'. Milton, banishing Melancholy, summoned the Graces.

> But come thou Goddess fair and free
> In heaven yclept Euphrosyne,
> And by men, heart-easing mirth,
> Whom lovely Venus at a birth
> With two Sister Graces more
> To ivy-crownéd Bacchus bore.

Christianity adopted the simple and serene word to mean the Divine Favour and the state of those enjoying it. Thence comes the meaning of favour generally. Shakespeare's Benedick puns on the two states of grace. 'Till all graces be in one woman, one woman shall not come in my grace.' Grace, as a favour or permission, lives on in University lingo. Next comes gratitude, at table or elsewhere. What a comprehensive word is this which first means the favour demanded and then the thankfulness of a recipient! Grace has drawn to itself all manner of fair visions and implications. It must not be abused by overwork.

GREENTH

ENGLAND is everlastingly praised for its greenery, though it is grey for more months than it is green. Certainly our spring and summer landscape offers countless varieties of green, for which the writer has sadly few terms. How he envies the painter when confronted with the spring-time subtleties of young larch, beech, and willow! Indeed, almost every tree runs to a different shade of what Horace Walpole called 'greenth'. Rejoicing to be home, after travel, and beside his darling Thames, he wrote,

> I do nothing but plume and clean myself and enjoy the verdure and silent waves. Neatness and greenth are so essential in my opinion to the country that in France, where I see nothing but chalk and dirty peasants, I seem in a terrestrial purgatory that is neither town nor country. The face of England is so beautiful that I do not believe Tempe or Arcadia were half so rural; for both lying in hot climates must have wanted the turf of our lawns.

Most Hellenic travellers will agree that he is wholly right about Arcadia and Tempe. English grass would seem a blessed miracle to a Greek peasant, sheep, or goat, especially in the Peloponnese. Greenth, Walpole's own coinage, is not beautiful, but somehow expresses the lush growth of a river valley better than does the cooler and more pleasant-sounding greenery. The English writer, as I said, is sorely limited in means to describe green things. The Latinities, verdant and virid, are chilly and formal.

HALCYON

THE Halcyon was supposed to nest on the sea-surface and to put a spell on the winds and waves, completely calming them in order that the nest might survive. This legend is especially connected with the waters round Sicily.

Alcyone was the daughter of Aeolus the wind-god and threw herself into the sea when a storm killed her husband. As a response to this sharp, daughterly reproach the gods turned the couple into kingfishers, who nested on the sea. Aeolus, now repentant, kept the waters tranquil for their breeding season. As Shelley observed,

The halcyons brood around the foamless isles,
The treacherous ocean has forsworn its wiles.

In any case, it is an exquisite word, passing on from tranquil weather to all benign and peaceful things. But Shakespeare thought of another aspect of kingfishers, when he mentioned the 'halcyon beaks' of servile, smiling rogues, which honest Kent so disliked to look upon. Halcyon here simply implies a long and sharp feature: in that case, we are all acquainted with a halcyon beak or two, but these are not necessarily limited to knaves and toadies.

HEBETUDE

HEBETUDE, both meaning by classical derivation and suggesting with its sound a dull heaviness, is now rare. It was used by A. E. Housman in his dismissal of inferior Latinists and Housman was never the kind of scholar to display nervous hesitation in the criticism of his fellow-classics. He brought 'hebetude' crashing down upon their skulls as though it were a lexicon itself. I regret its rarity, for it has a fine, ponderous expressiveness. Another classical rarity, concinnity, might well be restored to common use along with hebetude. It happens to be almost its opposite in meaning, since it signifies the skilful harmonizing of parts in thought and speech and so implies elegance of style. The first Lord Birkenhead, himself a relentless hammer of all hebetude, employed concinnity as a word and often displayed that quality in his quick forging of a sharp and shining phrase.

HESPERIDES

MANKIND from the earliest has looked westward for salvation: that is odd since the dawn, the obvious symbol of a new and better day, is not there. But the notion of Atlantis, of Blessed Isles, of a happy land beyond the evening star has been remarkably constant. America, by becoming the refuge of the pilgrim and the persecuted, the restless and the exile, naturally gave modern man new cause to favour the Hesperidean myth. The words Hesperus and Hesperides are themselves magnetic to the pens of poets and I can never see either without inclining to the old sentimental dream of some Paradise on the westering verge of great Oceanus.

> Love's tongue proves dainty Bacchus gross in taste:
> For valour, is not love a Hercules,
> Still climbing trees in the Hesperides?
> Subtle as sphinx; as sweet and musical
> As bright Apollo's lute, strung with his hair?
> And when love speaks, the voice of all the gods
> Makes heaven drowsy with the harmony.

Thus young Shakespeare's young Biron, flown with conceits and profligate of words. Those who like a vocabulary to be both inventive and irridescent can dip and dip again in *Love's Labour's Lost* and still come up with fresh discovery.

HOMELY

THE Englishman in America is warned not to call young women homely since there it means ugly instead of natural and simple. It is a charitably evasive usage which we might recover. I say 'recover' because, as usual, America has kept the original meaning which we have lost. The Pilgrim Fathers took 'homely', meaning unbeautiful, in their humble lexicon. Milton makes that certain. When Comus has given the lady his nicely-sounding plea for nudism,

> Beauty is nature's brag and must be shown

he continues,

> It is for homely features to keep home,
> They had their name thence; course complexions
> And cheeks of sorry grain will serve to ply

The sampler, and to teize the huswife's wooll.
What need a vermeil-tinctured lip for that
Love-darting eyes, or tresses like the Morn?

We need not accept the monster's belief that lip-stick lifts girls above the domesticities, but we English may well repatriate the ancient use of 'homely' which America has preserved to its profit.

HONEY

HONEY is a fair word of curious fortune. As an endearment it lingers more in America than in England, where it is most common in the form of 'hinny', a popular usage for darling in the North-East. (Hinny, in the live-stock lists, means the offspring of a she-ass by a stallion!) The favour shown to honey depends naturally on the sweetness of an epoch's tooth. Ours, whose taste is for the austere and stark and acid, would regard 'honey-tongued' as an adjective of contempt if applied to a contemporary poet. Yet, to the Tudor mind, this was the highest praise. It is noteworthy that the earliest contemporary allusions to Shakespeare nearly all relate him, with rapture, to the honey-pot. Spenser's

But that same gentle Spirit from whose pen
Large streames of honnie and sweete Nectar flowe

may or may not refer to Shakespeare, but it exemplifies the use of honey as a word of tribute. The same applies to Chettle's rebuke on a poet's silence at Elizabeth's death, a rebuke perhaps intended for William.

Nor doth the silver-tongued Melicert
Drop from his honied Muse one sable teare.

Meres (1598) was more specific. 'The sweete, wittie soule of Ovid lies in mellifluous and honey-tongued Shakespeare, witnes his Venus and Adonis, his Lucrece, his sugred Sonnets among his private friends.'

In the same year Richard Barnfield wrote

> And Shakespeare thou, whose hony-flowing Vaine
> (Pleasing the World) thy Praises doth obtaine.

In 1599 John Weever cried,

> Honie-tongued Shakespeare, when I saw thine issue
> I swore Apollo got them and no other.

In the 'Parnassus' Cambridge plays he is 'Sweet Mr. Shakespeare' and later on the 'nectared vein' is continually stressed. In Shakespeare's own work honey is often used, as noun and adjective, for exquisite things. But nowadays we hardly think of the author of *Hamlet* in terms of the honey-pot. For those who want an even more dulcet term of praise there is 'rodomel', which means the juice of rose-leaves mixed with honey and sings its way very happily into a line of the lusher poetry.

HORDE

THE history of horde is typical of the way in which we work words to death. It came to us from the Near East and first meant simply a nomad tribe with no suggestion of ferocity. Then it proceeded to imply savagery and next a large number of savages. Now horde is commonly, very commonly, employed to describe the enemy, suggesting both his myriads and his bestiality. Civil Servants, according to the Press, habitually move in hordes. 'A horde of highly-paid officials' is the modern variant of the Dickensian Barnacles. Since the war the Nazis have habitually been massing (only one's own side mobilizes) in hordes (only one's own side has millions of well-trained troops). One of the most striking instances of this usage in my recent experience was an article hopefully describing the millions of men in the Russian armies, who would far outnumber the Germans. None the less the latter were still described as moving in 'hordes' as though they were doing something particularly odious in being thus numerous — but not

71

quite so numerous as their enemies. Our allies, of course, had armies, not hordes.

HORRID

THE decline of horrid is lamentable. It should carry the idea of something bristling and frightful with a spiky menace and not merely be a mild term for nastiness. Vergil's 'Bella, horrida bella' sets spears and swords flashing in the air and does not refer only to the discomforts and incivilities of war. Milton is always exactly classical in his employment of such words. The Elder Brother in 'Comus', in the famous speech on Chastity, says that the owner of that virtue can traverse without harm 'Infamous hills' (i.e. unknown country) and pass

> where very Desolation dwells
> By grots and caverns shagged with horrid shades

unmenaced by goblin or 'swart faery of the mire'. Shakespeare, writing earlier than Milton, is none the less often closer to us in his usage. So it happens with horrid, which he applies vigorously to ghosts, night, thunder, speech, and hent. Hent, by the way, means to seize, or, as a noun, a seizing or design.

Horrible has suffered equal decline. When Cowper, musing on 'The Solitude of Alexander Selkirk', remarked

> Better dwell in the midst of alarms
> Than reign in this horrible place,

he meant something far more frightening than his adjective now implies. The same thing has happened in his next verse, which is made wellnigh ridiculous by the change of meaning in 'shocking'.

> The beasts that roam over the plain
> My form with indifference see;
> They are so unacquainted with man,
> Their tameness is shocking to me.

While on the subject of epithets in mutilation or decay, let me quote

72

this recent advertisement of a popular musical play: 'Terrific cast of 50.' That was meant to attract, not deter. Poor terrific!

HORTULAN

THIS adjective to signify of or pertaining to gardens is pure Latin and was used in the seventeenth and eighteenth centuries with some propriety, since the Palladian style of architecture was then the stately vogue and carried with its Italian splendours Italian notions of landscape-gardening. How elaborate those notions were can be seen from the syllabus to an intended book of John Evelyn's called *Elysium Britannicum*. Here are some of his projected chapters as cited by Miss Eleanour Sinclair Rohde and Mr. Eric Parker, most eager of hortulan anthologists.

'5. Of Knots, Parterres, Compartments, Borders, and Emboss-ments. — 6. Of Walks, Terraces, Carpets, and Alleys, Bowling-greens, Malls, their materials and proportions. — 7. Of Groves, Labyrinths, Daedales, Cabinets, Cradles, Pavilions, Galleries, Close-walks, and other Relievos. — 8. Of Transplanting. — 9. Of Fountains, Cascades, Rivulets, Piscinas, and Water-Works. — 10. Of Rocks, Grots, Cryptas, Mounts, Precipices, Porticos, Vendiducts. — 11. Of Statues, Columns, Dials, Perspectives, Pots, Vases, and other ornaments. — 12. Of Artificial Echos, Music, and Hydraulic mo-tions. — 13. Of Aviaries, Apiaries, Vivaries, Insects. — 14. Of Orangeries, and Conservatories of Rare Plants. — 15. Of Verdures, Perennial-Greens, and perpetual Springs. — 16. Of Coronary Gardens, Flowers, and rare Plants, how they are to be propagated, governed, and improved; together with a Catalogue of the choicest Trees, Shrubs, and Flowers, and how the Gardener is to keep his Register. — 17. Of the Philosophico-Medical Garden'.

'There's richness for you', as Mr. Squeers said of another matter. What, by the way, goes on in 'Philosophico-Medical' pleasaunces? Nowadays one can only think of an Open Air or Hortulan Brains Trust led by James Bridie and Oliver St. John Gogarty.

73

IMBRUE

HANDS stained with blood seem much more gory when imbrued. Pistol, sword in reluctant hand, made the word forever melodrama when he cried, in burlesque of his rival-mummers, 'What, shall we have incision? Shall we imbrue?' Bacchus, in Anglo-classical poetry, is continually imbrued with juice of the grape.

> And little rills of crimson wine imbrued
> His plump white arms and shoulders, enough white
> For Venus' pearly bite.

This is certainly not the happiest of Keats (no genius was more liable to bathos than his), but imbrued gives it what quality it has.

INCHOATE

AN imposing word and one almost as generally misused as fruition. Fruition's passage from meaning enjoyment in Marlowe to meaning fulfilment in modern political speeches and leading articles was caused by the simple fact that it began with the letters 'fruit'. The abuse of 'inchoate', which is properly applied to a thing just begun, is caused by a careless confusion with 'chaos'. The altered position of the vowels does not deter people from this muddle and politicians will announce that 'The Government's plans have now become utterly inchoate' which is to say that a boy has become a baby. 'Inchoate', is a good, resounding Latin word meaning incipient and was properly used by the judicious Hooker when he contrasted the inchoation of spiritual grace with its consummation.

INDIFFERENT

WORDS always seem to come down in the world and I have sought in vain for one that has risen in esteem, that is to say a word whose meaning has gone from slight to serious or indifferent to important. I mention indifferent because that is an example of the general process of decay. To Sir Philip Sidney it meant impartial and was an adjective of warmest praise when bestowed on justice. His description of sleep

> The indifferent judge between the high and low

is a tribute. To a modern it might merely suggest a judge who did not know his business. Shakespeare used indifferent in both senses (Sir Andrew says that his leg 'does indifferent well in a flame-coloured stock') and sometimes, characteristically, he blends the meanings. What exactly does Hamlet intend by 'I am myself indifferent honest'? Moderately honest or completely impartial? Respectable is a similar word which has suffered parallel devaluation. It was once an epithet of genuine praise. To call a general a respectable soldier was to say that all looked up to his abilities. Now it implies that nobody looks up to him at all. Respectable is slightly kinder than indifferent, but it is not welcomed. David Garrick would have liked to be called a respectable actor by a critic: now an actor thus described would feel himself aggrieved. The gradual segregation of respectability for a rather dull kind of piety has worked some of the damage. It is strange how shy is man of having virtue thrust upon him.

INFINITE

INFINITE is not in itself an attractive word, but it occurs in some of the most powerful passages of English poetry. This, as F. L. Lucas points out in his admirable edition of John Webster's plays, is due to Renaissance absorption in the enormous mystery of creation. The conception of size, of boundless and eternal things, was a splendour in their minds. The idea of the colossal allured those fiery particles who built English poetry by marrying the vernacular to the new learning and Latinity from the East. The Hitlerite cry of him who was to be Richard III,

> To undertake the death of all the world,

is the very voice of an ambition which will have nothing but the universal. It sounds like Marlowe, who constantly utters this same passion for the endless and the absolute. Webster plays continually with infinity. It occurs in a tribute of devotion.

> Had I infinite worlds
> They were too little for thee.

It spreads its misty magic over this marvellous farewell to life.

> I am i' the way to study a long silence;
> To prate were idle, I remember nothing;
> There's nothing of so infinite vexation
> As man's own thoughts.

(The first line is surely the perfect last line of a dying actor.) Infinite is often on the lips of Hamlet and both describes and voices the fascination and the longings of Cleopatra. She cries to Antony,

> O infinite virtue, come'st thou smiling from
> The world's great snare uncaught?

and, at the end, we know

> She hath pursued conclusions infinite
> Of easy ways to die.

Death and black cypress and minds forlornly ranging 'beyond the infinite of thought' are the background of Elizabethan fifth acts. Almost a mean word to the ear is infinite, but it keeps majestic company.

INGENIOUS

THIS good word should be restored to its ancient and honourable estate, whereby it implies possession of intellect or genius and not just a species of inventive cunning. To the men of the Renaissance Italy was essentially 'Ingenious Italy'. Carelessness has also muddled this word with ingenuous, which means nobly-born and then honest, straightforward. Shakespeare was in error over this. Timon's 'Ingeniously, I speak' should obviously be 'Ingenuously'. (Perhaps Shakespeare was right and his printers wrong.) However, the error became so general that our word 'ingenuity', which ought to mean straightforwardness, is now always used for a light kind of cleverness, as though it were the noun of the adjective 'ingenious'. There is a case here for some tidying.

JINK

JINKS, like dudgeon previously noted, are now always high. Jink, verb or noun, is a Scots word and a lively one for a lively process. Escaping Scotsmen jink their creditors, the jink being a quick side-step. If the word is not used of footballers, it should be, for jinking is an exact term for the elusive footwork and swerve of a great runner with the ball. 'Our billie's gien us a' the jink', wrote Burns of one who had flitted overseas. Apparently at the card-table jinking means 'winning a game of spoil-five, twenty-five, or forty-five'. This sport is beyond my ken.

So, says Oxford, jinks pass on to signify 'various frolics at drinking parties'. And there, as we have seen, height appears to be the inseparable quality of jinks. These matters of measurement are queer. High jinks go with low company.

Jinking during the war was a term much used in the Royal Air Force for dodging anti-aircraft fire by rapid moves this way and that.

JUGULATE

MAY we admit words which are only attractive if misused? We frowned on the mistaken fruition and praised its proper application. Perhaps, for once, we may reverse that process. Jugulate ought to mean 'cut the throat of', in which case it is a direct, rather ugly, Latinized, surgical term. But Thackeray, very happily, applied it to a lady's singing which he much disliked. He was obviously thinking in terms of Nash's ditty of avian spring-song with its refrain of 'Cuckoo, jug-jug, pu-we, to-witta-woo'. Thackeray's confusion has certainly given us an aptly descriptive word. We have all of us encountered sopranos for whom jugulation is a proper term.

THIS is an ugly Latinism, but interesting. It means, of course, a meeting or union, but modern usage has reserved junction for that and now quite commonly applies juncture to a moment of time. First important events converged so that it was reasonable to talk of a 'critical juncture'. The phrase was striking and, like so many striking phrases, became an overworked cliché. Every careless writer began to use 'At this juncture' when he simply meant 'then'. I was reminded of this by finding the word used by Gilbert White of Selborne in a passage where it could refer both to a moment of time and an act of union. He was writing of the mating of swifts and claimed that swifts 'tread, or copulate, on the wing'. (Tread is a technical and descriptive term of avian amours.) The swift, he explained with that stately stride of his prose which is like good, supple walking,

> is almost continually on the wing; and as it never settles on the ground, on trees, or roofs, would seldom find opportunity for amorous rites, was it not enabled to indulge them in the air. If any person would watch these birds of a fine morning in May, as they are sailing round at a great height from the ground, he would see, every now and then, one drop on the back of another, and both of them sink down together for many fathoms with a loud piercing shriek. This I take to be the juncture when the business of generation is carrying on.
>
> As the swift eats, drinks, collects materials for its nest, and, as it seems, propagates on the wing; it appears to live more in the air than any other bird, and to perform all functions there save those of sleeping and incubation.

Juncture is rarely used with such aptitude to both its meanings.

KITTLE

KITTLE means tickle, possibly by confusion of the two sounds, both of which are based on the light noise of the action itself. So one kittled the strings of a violin. Curiously both verbs are used in the same way as adjectives, meaning difficult or risky. We all know that women are 'kittle cattle' and golfers, with any sense of language, know the terrors of greens that are kittle. Tickle, which now seems much more delicate than ticklish because the latter has been so much used of purely physical reactions, occurs in Sir Walter Raleigh's great poem 'The Lie'.

> Tell wit how much it wrangles
>   In tickle points of nyceness,
> Tell wisedome she entangles
>   Her selfe in over wiseness,
> And when they doe reply
>   Straight give them both the lie.

It was good legal English of the Elizabethans to 'stand upon a tickle point'.

LEATHERY

LEATHER is a poor word for a substance that can be so handsome. Leather ought to burnish our poetry far more than it does. But our Horseback Halls, so much less articulate and so much more frequent than our Heartbreak Houses, have never sufficiently voiced their own beauties. It has always been the metals that made the music and the glitter; the swords, not the saddles, romantically gleam. So leathery things are usually left to prose or the paint-box of Mr. Munnings. As if there were no lyrics lurking in a stable! There are, of course, and Mr. John Betjeman fetches them out, as in his lines on Upper Lambourne.

> Leathery limbs of Upper Lambourne,
>   Leathery skin from sun and wind,
> Leathery breeches, spreading stables,
>   Shining saddles left behind,
> To the down the string of horses
>   Moving out of sight and mind.

There is a large piece of England in the several stanzas of that shining poem.

LEWD

A QUEER, revolting, and therefore apt little word is lewd. It originally meant a layman, unclerical, and therefore unread. From that it came to signify vulgar and base in general and was rapidly annexed for a single species of evil. Lewd, by Shakespeare's time, is nearly always used of sexual unpleasantness. The Biblical translators, with their 'lewd fellows of the baser sort', may not have been thinking only of the lecherous, but the horrid little word was being strongly tilted in that direction and has remained so. Once meaning the ignorant it is now applied rather to the precocity which knows too much. In a subsequent note it will be observed how the English words for strong and stubborn all seem to begin with 'st'. A similar curious thing occurs in the case of sexual debauchery. Here 'l' is the favoured initial. Lewd, lecherous, libidinous, loose, lustful — they make a loathsome addition to the tranquil propriety of love. Another which might have been added to this rakish company is luxury, since that to the Elizabethans meant sexual indulgence and not the appurtenances of a costly hotel. Now luxury has come up in the world and is applied rather to caviare than to chambering. (When did the phrase 'lap of luxury' first appear and had it a sexual significance then?) A cinema 'de luxe' (or 'de loo' as the really refined have been known to call it) now only suggests pile carpets, fountains with goldfish and more nutritive fountains of ice cream, padded 'fotiles', and usherettes in pyjamas. To Shakespeare it would have meant a picture-house with a brothel attached. 'Fye on lust and luxury' sing the fairies pinching Falstaff at the close of *The Merry Wives of Windsor*. This does not suggest that the Garter Hotel, Windsor, was the Grand Babylon of its day, but merely that Sir John had been behaving as a nasty old man: in short, as Mistress Page observed, he was 'a lewdster'.

LOVE

'FROM weak grade of Teutonic root leub' and so linked with the Indo-European lubido. English has softened this simple and inclusive word which covers all yearning from strongest passion to tenderest affection, and then wanders off to mean a game of cards or 'no score' at lawn-tennis. It is sometimes claimed that the Tudor poets, who so enchantingly used it, pronounced it as north-country folk do still, luv. Either way, it does well. To fall in love is a fair phrase, as simple as the actual process and as pleasant. The strange thing about the vocabulary of passion is the inadequacy of the words for love's fulfilling. The commonest in use is a mean and ugly monosyllable which is not fit even to be an oath, while the correct and printable are heavy and dull. Copulate and cohabit sound as little attractive as a laboratory or legal process. Fornicate, for less legitimate pleasures, is a most unlovely word which comes out of the brothel. The Biblical 'Chambering and wantoning' has a less deterrent sound and does at least suggest enjoyment. The lowest depth of pitiful insufficiency in language was reached by a young man whom I heard using sex as a verb of the active mood. So we come back gladly to the brief, comprehensive, and fair-sounding love.

MADRIGAL

LET the scholars argue over the ultimate origin of this lovely alien. The O. E. D. traces it back through Italy to the Greek word for a fold and says 'a pastoral song'. Morrison Boyd in his *Elizabethan Music*, following E. H. Fellowes, affirms, as seems more probable, that it simply means 'a composition in the mother tongue'. We can leave the etymology to the specialists. It is more generally important that the Renaissance wafted the madrigal to England where it flourished exceedingly under such masters as Byrd, Downham, Farnaby, Gibbons, Morley and other leaders of that enchanting choir. 'A madrigal was a secular composition for unaccompanied voices (two to eight) each singing a separate part.' Five voices were common and common too was a theme of love. Gilbert and Sullivan have made us think of the madrigal as 'merry', but the Elizabethan's addiction to melancholy admitted sighs and groans and 'dumps' to this form of writing. Madrigal, because of its exquisite sound, naturally passed into general poetic usage as a synonym for all sweetness of sound. Marlowe's Passionate Shepherd calling,

> Come live with me and be my love
> And we will all the pleasures prove

invites to a session

> By shallow rivers, to whose falls
> Melodious birds sing madrigals.

After that madrigals go ringing down the aisles of English poetry and might be said to ring the bells of heaven too, when Henley called the Wren spires of London's city 'madrigals in stone'.

MAGAZINE

A MAGAZINE comes, by way of France, out of Araby. It has in its time meant any kind of store from a dairy (magazine of milk and butter, Defoe), to an arsenal. Charles Cotton, in a gay little song defying winter, described his resources for the campaign.

> There, under ground, a magazine
> Of sovran juice is cellar'd in:
> Liquor that will the siege maintain,
> Should Phoebus ne'er return again.

James Thomson inquired of the winds,

> Where are your stores, ye powerful beings, say,
> Where your aerial magazines reserved
> To swell the brooding terrors of the storm?

In the later eighteenth century the word added to its general utility by taking on its now common literary meaning. By 'Magazine of Taste' you might expect to find described one of the glossier and more expensive fashion-journals. But this magnificent phrase was, in fact, the title of a dining-room utensil popular a century ago. This was a super-cruet, containing all possible condiments, 'zests' and sauces, and carried the proud, proprietary title of 'Dr. Kitchener's Magazine of Taste'. To remark 'May I trouble you, Sir Eustace, for the Magazine?' did not imply a churlish desire to read at table, but only an interest in added savours.

MANSE AND MANSION

MANSION once meant, according to its Latin origin, any 'remaining-place', a country as well as a house. Then it developed a special meaning on the medieval stage, whose 'mansions' were the separate sections or apartments signifying different spheres of heaven, hell, and earth. The famous but strange-seeming line, 'In My Father's house are many mansions', is explained by this usage. The Scottish form 'manse' is a beautiful word and though, as applied to the minister's dwelling, it has often been a Bleak House in puritanical fact, it comes most softly and sweetly to the ear. The English poets might have seized it. Instead they have realized the rhythmical value and slightly celestial implications of the longer word. Housman began his hymn 'For My Funeral' with,

> O thou that from thy mansion,
> Through time and place to roam,
> Dost send abroad thy children
> And then dost call them home.

Emily Dickinson, vividly creative in her use of words, had 'Summer's nimble mansion'. It is indeed a pity that the Victorian 'real estate men' snatched and assassinated mansion when they started to build what we call 'flats' and Americans 'apartments'.

MARGARINE

YES, margarine, with the 'g' hard, is a beautiful word and much the same as Margaret, for both come out of Greece and mean pearl or pearly. Unfortunately for margarine it has been usurped to signify legally 'any substitute for butter made from oleomargarine' and can be used for all substances made in imitation of butter and offered for sale. The stuff was once an oily horror and that has damned a fair word in a foul mess. A revengeful public degraded margarine to 'marge'. But science has so far bettered margarine as to make it often preferable to a dubious butter and so we owe the word some compensation. Butter is a good, fat word, but unlovely. 'He asked for butter and she brought forth milk. She brought forth butter in a lordly dish.' Margarine has far more delicacy and, if we could only refer it back to its jewelled origins, might take its place in poetry. With its pearly connotation and with 'g' kept hard, it could certainly stand in limpid Tennysonian numbers.

> The sky was azure, flecked with margarine,

or

> Fair Margaret in silk of margarine

might have resounded well in a revival of Victorian modes. But the laboratory and the grocer have put an end to all that.

MEAGRE

MEAGRE began by signifying a thin person and proceeded later to describe the diet likely to make him so. In Chaucer the man is meagre, in Lamb the banquet. As applied to an invalid the adjective can have a pallid, haunting vividness. Milton has

> Blue, meager hag or stubborn unlaid ghost.

Again, there is

> Thou shalt see the field-mouse peep
> Meagre from its cellèd sleep.

Thus Keats on the tim'rous beastie. The most poignant usage of
meagre that I know occurs in Shakespeare's *King John* during Queen
Constance's superb lament for the doomed Prince Arthur.

> There was not such a gracious creature born.
> But now will canker sorrow eat my bud,
> And chase the native beauty from his cheek,
> And he will look as hollow as a ghost,
> As dim and meagre as an ague's fit;
> And so he'll die;

The Queen then goes on to the majestic cry,

> Grief fills the room up of my absent child,
> Lies in his bed, walks up and down with me,
> Puts on his pretty looks, repeats his words,
> Remembers me of all his gracious parts,
> Stuffs out his vacant garments with his form;
> Then have I reason to be fond of grief.

In connection with these lines one has to remember that *King John*
was written, fairly certainly, late in 1596. In August 1596 Shakespeare's only son, Hamnet, died in Stratford-on-Avon, aged eleven.
We do not know the cause, but that the boy looked at the end

> As dim and meagre as an ague's fit

is all too likely. If ever a poet wrote after personal loss and from a
riven heart, surely it was here.

MEW

WHY have we let slip a word so apt for all sorts of confinement
and restriction?

> For aye to be in shady cloister mew'd,
> To live a barren sister all your life,
> Chanting faint hymns to the cold, fruitless moon,

is Theseus' well-known threat to Hermia. The brief, expressive, melancholy word fits beautifully into all such pictures of the cloister without a hearth. Mewing, originally, meant penning up a falcon while it moulted, or setting a fowl apart for fattening. But it was lifted for larger matters of human imprisonment, as Juliet was 'mew'd up to her heaviness'. It is rather a sad comment on the rigours of Elizabethan life that with their mewing and cribbing and cabining they have so rich a vocabulary for so bleak a subject.

MICHING

MICHING is skulking, hiding, or thieving. Perhaps Herrick had both shades of meaning in mind when he wrote

> A cat
> I keep, that plays about my house,
> Grown fat
> With eating many a miching mouse.

Hamlet's 'Miching mallecho' is usually interpreted as secret mischief.

'Shall the blessed sun of heaven prove a micher and eat black-berries?' asked Falstaff, thinking rather of trespass.

The same poem of Herrick's, by the way, has a curious verb for the fruitful hen.

> A hen
> I keep, which, creeking day by day,
> Tells when
> She goes her long white egg to lay.

Herrick, like Clare, two centuries later, is a great minter of words. Out of his treasury tumble ancient and modern pieces. His 'Once a virgin flosculet', for example, is a very classical bud, but Herrick sometimes sets Latin moving on tip-toe instead of using the heavy Roman tread.

THIS is a joke-word and possibly has no business here. Certainly no dictionary has knowledge of it. But it could be very usefully employed, especially to 'de-gas' a certain type of intellectual blimp-ishness (for surely there can be blimps of cerebration as of the reverse) and so I offer it for adoption. I owe it to the dramatist, John Van Druten, who some years ago passed it on to me as an 'Initial' Word, composed of the first letters of Mind Over Matter. Far be it from me to dethrone the brain from its proper sovereignty over body: what Mom signifies is not a due regard for reason, but all the Thought that is High with a capital 'H' and all the Minded-ness that is Right with a capital 'R'. It curtly summarizes the tire-some people who believe that they are mystics simply because they are mystified and claim to be on a higher plane than most of us because their minds are in a far greater mess. They appear to choose words by their length and opinions by their muddle. To say of these that they are 'terribly Mom' is often as just as it is expressive.

MONSTER

A MONSTER, from being a divine portent, came to mean any-thing unnatural. It is not necessarily large. Indeed, the word seems unusually vivid when preceded by the adjective 'little'. Monster as a noun-epithet for anything vast is a usage of modern journalism, which has to keep on the high note and pretend that any big gathering is a 'monster-meeting'. The adjective monstrous has been worked to death, but the substantive has still virtue in it. The Loch Ness Monster, for example, seemed to me much more impressive and frightening than any Dragon or Apparition of Loch Ness. The word can be most effectively used as any contrast to reality. The old dramatists had graceful epilogues instead of the limping after-curtain speech whose wearisome distribution of 'credits' is a curse of 'first-nights' in our time. One of the best of such tributes by an author to his colleagues is that at the end of

Webster's *The White Devil*, whose prologue, incidentally, puts
Shakespeare in his place as one of many approved and not as the
genius 'out-topping knowledge' of later opinion. Here is the
epilogue:

> For the action of the play (i.e. acting) 'twas generally well
> done and I dare affirme, with joint testimony of some of their
> own quality, (for the true imitation of life without striving to
> make nature a monster) the best that ever became them;
> whereof, as I make a generall acknowledgement, so in par-
> ticular I must remember the well-approved industry of my
> friend Maister Perkins and confesse the worth of his action did
> Crowne both the beginning and the end.

The dramatists of that time were ever nervous lest the actor,
deserting nature, should play the monster. But Webster certainly
gave the play-boys encouragement. For some of his characters are
pretty near to being monsters themselves — as well as having
'monstrous fine' things to say.

MUSHROOM

MOSS is a good soft word for a good soft thing. (It were much
better if London's hill of the Mosswell had not been hardened into
our ugly Muswell) and Mushroom is one of its products, most
charming in its early form 'mush-rump'. It is queer to discover that
our use of mushroom for an upstart is as old as the sixteenth century.
Then one would have expected it to refer only to a tasty fungus
growing among fairy circles.

There is always a suggestion of magic about mushrooms, so swift
and so nocturnal in their coming. 'Sleeker than night-swollen
mushrooms' are the heifers in 'Endymion'. It is right that Shakespeare's magician, Prospero, should be the only one of his characters
to mention mushrooms. One imagines Rosalind's Arden and
Oberon's Athens to be full of them. But Shakespearean mushrooms grow only where Ariel has trod.

NAPPY

LIQUORS, like cloth, have their nap. So nappy is a foamy beer, stuff with a head to it. It is mainly thought of as Scottish now, since Burns had it often on his lips.

> While we sit sousing at the nappy,
> And gettin' foo and unco' happy.

Later in 'Tam o' Shanter' the beer has become 'swats', another good toss-pot word.

> Fast by an ingle, bleezing finely,
> Wi' reaming swats, that drank divinely.

But the nappy is good Tudor English too. Campion, writing in the courtiers' conventional but not always convincing praise of the cottar's Saturday night, sang of his Jack and Joan,

> Well can they judge of nappy ale ·
> And tell at large a winter's tale.

Shakespeare makes no use of it, but the word foams freely about the tankards and verses of his time.

NESH

NESH, for tender and susceptible (especially to hard climate) lingers on in country dialect. It is the kind of simple and vivid word which one might expect to be rediscovered by a probing genius, like Cecil Sharp, along with English folk songs and dances in mid-America whither it had been carried in some pilgrim's pack. It used also to have a contemptuous significance, hinting at poltroonery. 'Sitting ower t' fire makes a body nesh', says the northern farmer. But it is essentially a tender-sounding word and should be tenderly restored to the service of tender people and of delicate things.

NOSEGAY

'THERE be some flowers make a delicious Tussie-Mussie or Nosegay both for sight and smell.' Thus John Parkinson, a herbalist of the early seventeenth century. Tussie-Mussie was too good to be lost, but lost it seems to have been. The charming simplicity of nosegay remains, though nostrils are certainly less sensitive to fine aromas owing to smoking. (Tobacco does more to weaken sense of smell than sense of taste.) Nosegay was fairly common in Tudor English, whose lovers 'said it with flowers' and with other things.

> With bracelets of thy hair, rings, gawds, conceits,
> Knacks, trifles, nosegays, sweetmeats —

There are the Shakespearean tokens and tribute of adoration. Shakespeare applied 'posy' only to verse — it is simply a shortening of poesy — and this usage is now extinct. But posy, as a bunch of flowers instead of as a bunch of flower-like words, was familiar to Marlowe and posies have gone on rhyming with roses ever since he wedded them.

OBSEQUIOUS AND OFFICIOUS

A LONG list might be made of terms which have gone down hill. Both these words, for example, have somehow acquired a bad name. Both rightly mean dutiful, but obsequious was degraded to mean over-humble and so fawning, while officious was employed for over-busy and so fussy and meddlesome. Both are to be found in their state of innocence in the poetry of the seventeenth century. George Wither, for example, sang,

> When, with a serious musing I behold,
> The grateful and obsequious Marygold,
> How duly, every morning, she displays
> Her open breast, when Titan spreads his rays,

while Marvell, moved by silver in darkness as Wither by the bloom of gold in day, cried,

> Ye glow-worms, whose officious flame
> To wandering mowers shows the way,
> That in the night have lost their aim
> And after foolish fires do stray,
> Your courteous lights in vain you waste . . .

Milton called the stars 'Bright luminaries Officious' and Dryden frequently used officious to signify serviceable. In his Panegyric on the Coronation of Charles II he wrote,

> Now charged with blessings while you seek repose
> Officious slumbers haste your eyes to close.

It would be an obsequious and officious action to restore these good words to their former state of honour.

ODDLING

The O. E. D. knows nothing of oddling, a word which pleases me by its double suggestion of the lonely and the queer. (Ben Jonson's odling, which probably means cozening, is another matter altogether.) Oddling seems to be the perfect word for certain types mainly to be discovered of old in winter-time, sitting in seaside hotels when patrons are few and prices low, or watching February seas from the shelter on the deserted esplanade. I first met it in John Clare's lines, as sombrely beautiful as woods in December, called 'Emmonsail's Heath in Winter'. He uses it of crows in the plural and one pictures a brace of peevish solitaries whom spring may render more mutually sympathetic.

> I love to see the old heath's withered brake
> Mingle its crimpled leaves with furze and ling,
> While the old heron from the lonely lake
> Starts slow and flaps his melancholy wing,
> And oddling crows in idle motions swing
> On the half rotten ashtree's topmost twig,
> Beside whose trunk the gipsy makes his bed.

A few lines later he has 'and coy bumbarrels twenty in a drove'. Mr. H. J. Massingham's editorial note in *Poems about Birds* explains 'bumbarrel' as a long-tailed tit, a rustic beauty of a word for an all too rare and beautiful species. Clare, that embodiment of East Midland earth, a piece of heathland animate, spills words in handsome plenty as he wanders across his simple fields and wastes.

OOZE

AN ugly word, but expressive. Nowadays it suggests slime and sluggish brown water or a slow trickle of some probably unpleasant fluid. But Shakespeare used it several times of the sea, mainly of thick water on the bottom, and Shelley followed him when he described the submarine forest of seaweed as,

> The sea blooms and the oozy woods which wear
> The sapless foliage of the ocean.

Dryden said of Father Thames 'Deep in his ooze he sought his sedgy bed', thus distinguishing between the water (ooze) and the muddy bottom. Ariel was wont to 'tread the ooze of the salt deep' and one thinks of that sprite treading only a cleanly moisture. Pericles, in an almost certainly Shakespearean passage of the play called after him, talks of throwing a coffin in the sea and here calls the sea 'ooze'. Perhaps ooze is now damned and muddied o'er beyond redemption. But, before I leave the word, I would like to give it my salute by suggesting a Shakespearean emendation which would lift ooze on to a peak of poetry. What did Macbeth mean when he cried,

> This my hand will rather
> The multitudinous seas incarnadine,
> Making the green one red?

Two theories are advanced. One, the least likely, that he meant making the Green One (i.e. the sea) red. Two, that 'one red' stands for 'all red'. But does either sound in the least like Tudor English? Are there parallels for such handling of the words? I suggest,

Making the green ooze red.

The printer's error in setting one instead of ooze is a much smaller one than many in the First Folio. Ooze here is not, I admit, altogether euphonious. But, with ooze as a noun, the sense is good, and you may take it alternatively as a verb, since Shakespeare employs it so. Either way the usage is truly Shakespearean. Let me confess that I have never found any support for this verbal hazard of mine. But I still believe in it.

OVER-GRIEVING

THE combination of 'v' and 'r' is often both melodious and powerful. The word grief, simple and common, is itself a gem, far more effective on the lips than pain or woe, and well-matched with sorrow, where again the 'r' is playing its emotional tricks. Grief is one of the words which almost make a line of poetry before the poet has begun. Listen to it in James Logie Robertson's masterpiece of accurate moderation concerning the Scottish climate. (It should be explained for the benefit of the English that 'aye' means always.)

> It's no aye rainin' on the misty Achils,
>   It's no aye white wi' winter on Nigour;
> The winds are no sae mony sorrowing Rachels,
>   That grieve, and o' their grief will no' gie owre.

There is a kind of unintentional humour (far from dry) about lines one and two. The Scotsman is having no poetic licence with the rainfall on the way to Gleneagles. No false claims for him. It will really stop raining sometime. Lines three and four have the music of the stormy hills. Trust the 'w's, 'r's and 'v's for that. The title of this Scottish variant on the Horatian 'non semper imbres' is 'Hughie seeks to console a Brother Shepherd, over-grieving for the loss of his Son'. 'Over-grieving', with its play of 'r's and 'v's, is excellent. There is good use of climatic grief in Browning's

What I love best in all the world
Is a castle, precipice-encurled,
In the heart of the wind-grieved Apennine.

Wind-grieved for heights is as good as 'wuthering'.

OVERWEEN

OVERWEEN now smacks of history-book English. 'The king, in
his overweening pride', etc. In these days it is always pride that
overweens, but there were times when people did their own
overweening, that is to say looked and carried themselves arro-
gantly, and the word might well be restored to the sense in which
Aubrey used it of Gwin, the Earl of Oxford's secretary.

> A better instance of a squeamish, disobligeing, slighting,
> insolent, proud fellow perhaps can't be found. . . . No reason
> satisfies him but he overweenes, and cutts some sower faces
> that would turn the milke in a fair ladie's breast.

There was no quicker portrait-painter than Aubrey. He could
make a word do a page's work.

PARADISE

PARADISE is simply a transliteration of the Greek word for a
park. Parks are still, to many town children, paradisal and park in
Scotland is still the meadow-land of a croft or farm. That bleak
and dusty horror, a car-park, has presumably destroyed the short
word's attraction, but the longer Paradise, though sometimes
sicklied with the worst kind of unction that religiosity distils, is a
grand word upon the lips. The letter 'r' is so often a comforter, in
the old sense of that word which I have already recorded and always
enjoy. The last line of a sonnet is safe with the roll of paradise in
its rhythm and rhyme. Siegfried Sassoon's

Remembrance of all beauty that has been
And stillness from the pools of Paradise,

suggests its magic. I was early taught by a man who had endured
a long and crippling illness. To him, at last able to sit in his garden,
the simple lines of Gray were truth indeed.

See the wretch that long has tost
On the thorny bed of pain,
At length repair his vigour lost
And breathe and walk again:
The meanest floweret of the vale,
The simplest note that swells the gale,
The common sun, the air, the skies,
To him are opening Paradise.

The sentiment is not trite to those who have suffered. I have not
forgotten the light in his eye as he spoke the verse and the surging
relish of Paradise upon his tongue. The Catholic martyr, Robert
Southwell, in the beautiful lines beginning

Christ's thorne is sharpe, no head His garland weares

used imparadise as a verb.

Sweet volumes, stoared with learning fit for saints,
Where blissful quires imparadise the mind.

Could there be a finer description of what is sometimes called by
Auctioneers a 'Gentleman's Library'?

PAVAN

PAVAN is the peacock-dance, a grave and stately measure, elabor-
ately costumed, another gift to England of the Renaissance.
The 'smash-hit' of early seventeenth century music was John
Dowland's pavan 'Lachrymae' with its modishly melancholic
numbers.

95

> Hark you shadows that in darkness dwell,
>   Learn to contemn light,
> Happy, happy they that in hell
>   Feel not the world's despite.

Those Jacobean 'blues' were certainly deeper and darker than ours —
and more dignified. Also their popular tunes had a longer life.
The popularity of 'Lachrymae' was still a play-house jest in 1624,
although Dowland had published it in 1605. It appeared thus:

> Lachrymae or Seaven Teares, Figured in Seaven Passionate
> Pavans with Divers Other Pavans, Galiards, and Almands, set
> forth for the Lutes, Viols, or Violons, in five parts.

A Galiard was a brisk dance, the epithet galiard (more commonly
galliard) still being in use as an equivalent to gallant. Sir Toby asked
Sir Andrew why he did not go to church in a galliard and come
home in a coranto. Almand or Almaine was, of course, a German
step. Robert Dowland in his 'Varietie of Lute-Lessons' listed
'Fantasies, Pavins, Galliards, Almains, Corantoes, and Volts'. The
two last were the running and the leaping dance. Says the Duke of
Bourbon in *Henry V*,

> They bid us to the English dancing-schools
> And teach lavoltas high and swift corantos.

Shakespeare is here assuming too much for his own country and
even playing at annexation. It was Italy that taught England both
to show a leg and charm the ear, and most musical was the
vocabulary of her instruction.

PAVILION

THE English cricketers did well to annex this butterfly term for
their premises, whether those be a humble shanty by a village field
or the august, metropolitan temple of the M.C.C. It is now a
graceful, green-and-white sort of word and rides easily in a world of
flannels and smooth turf. But the poets in the past have linked

pavilions with more martial and majestic things. The Hymnal has claimed this canopy for heaven and praised 'Our Shield and Defender, the Ancient of Days, Pavilioned in Splendour and girded with Praise'. Shakespeare, whenever he imagined a tented field was prodigal of 'brave pavilions' and naturally Cleopatra, first meeting Antony, was couched in a pavilion on that glittering and scented barge which 'burned upon the river'. All good makers of a lyric have seized on the word's musical possibilities and Francis Thompson sang 'the red pavilions of the heart'.

PEEK

PEEKING, for peering or spying, is another of the old English words which have retained their vitality in America, where a popular magazine can be called *Peek* to suggest its powers of scrutiny. The title would, I think, merely mystify the average customer at a London bookstall. That is a pity, for it is a nicely descriptive word and well suggests a sharp eye above a peering nose. I found it vividly employed in *A True Narrative and Relation of His Majesty's Miraculous Escape from Worcester in September, 1651.* Charles II, 'on the run', was hiding in the oak at Boscobel, guarded by the faithful family of Penderel. 'William and his wife Joan were ever peeking up and down.' Peep, which survives in common use, once served for celestial vision (cf. Vaughan's 'So some strange thoughts transcend our wonted themes, And into glory peep') and now is applied to small and gentle glimpses. The hard 'k' in peek is excellent for a tougher kind of observation and patrol-work. Peeping Toms should really be peekers. Keeking is common Scots for the same kind of thing, from Allan Ramsay to the crofters' lingo of to-day.

PERDU

PERDU, one lost or at least one of whom hope is mainly abandoned, was an ironic Elizabethan term for a soldier with a stiff place to hold.

Then it came to mean any kind of sentinel, without suggestion that the task was extremely hazardous. To Fuller shepherds are 'perdues in defence of their flocks' and the word crops up prettily in the lyrics of the seventeenth century. Cordelia applied it to old Lear's exposure.

> Was this a face
> To be opposed against the warring winds,
> To stand against the dread, deep-bolted thunder,
> In the most terrible and nimble stroke
> Of quick, cross lightning? To watch — poor perdu! —
> With this thin helm?

and Suckling has it in a parody of Shakespeare's early and sensuous vein. He is describing, in the manner of 'Lucrece', a lady couched.

> Out of the bed the other fair hand was
>   On a green satin quilt, whose perfect white
> Looked like a daisy in a field of grass
>   And showed like unmelt snow unto the sight:
> There lay the pretty perdue, safe to keep,
> The rest of the body that lay fast asleep.

Perdu seems now to be lost to the English language, to which it was a graceful immigrant. One of its modern equivalents in desperate gallantry is the 'Tail-End Charlie' who volunteers to be rear-gunner in a bombing aeroplane.

PEREGRINE

THIS term for a traveller or alien has almost dropped out. It is now limited to the peregrine falcon, who is not an alien, but certainly peregrinates the air with a compelling beauty and swooping magnificence of wing. Peregrinate is both Tudor verb and Tudor epithet. Shakespeare's schoolmaster, Holofernes, thus describes the Spaniard, Armado:

his humour is lofty, his discourse peremptory, his tongue

filed, his eye ambitious, his gait majestical, and his general
behaviour vain, ridiculous, and thrasonical. He is too picked,
too spruce, too affected, too odd, as it were, too peregrinate,
as I may call it,

to which the curate, Sir Nathaniel, adds 'A most singular and choice
epithet'.

Holofernes was a pedant and to use now, in his method, such fine-
sounding and polysyllabic terms as thrasonical and peregrinate
might savour of pretentiousness. But the shorter 'peregrine' is a
handsome word and would be a courteous welcome to a stranger.

PICKTHANK

I CAME across pickthank in Sir Thomas Browne, who wrote of
'pickthank delators', i.e. fawning informers. A pickthank fellow is
one who would steal your gratitude and a very good term it is. I
was the more surprised to find so blunt a piece of Saxon in Sir
Thomas, whose lexicon was mainly compounded of a grand
Latinity. From Rome he took his delator; from his own London
came pickthank. Shakespeare's Prince Hal has it too: he complains
of the 'smiling pickthanks and base newsmongers'. Biron in *Love's
Labour's Lost* comes very near to it with his disdain of

Some carry-tale, some please-man, some slight zany.
Some mumble-news, some trencher-knight, some Dick.

How feeble our modern 'yes-man' seems beside this roll-call of
the sycophants. Sir Walter Scott also used pickthank with effect in
dialogue.

PINCHBECK AND NOSTRUM

POLITICS afford a particular haunt for clichés. As an example of
the epithet that survives in a moribund state and only in one connection is 'pinchbeck', which scarcely ever appears nowadays without a
following 'Napoleon'. But how many of the scribes who have

dismissed Hitler or Mussolini or any upstart fellow who happens to sit on the wrong political bench as a 'pinchbeck Napoleon' could explain the term? Pinchbeck, as a matter of fact, is a town in Lincolnshire, and so gave a place-name to one Christopher Pinchbeck, a watchmaker who was skilled in the use of a certain alloy of copper and zinc which had the look of gold. Hence 'pinchbeck' comes to be used for 'false', and was so applied by Thackeray to a lady's golden tresses. But now there is only one kind of pinchbeck — namely, the Napoleonic — and its special habitat is righteous, democratic indignation.

The same kind of leader-writer, in the days of party politics, had the astonishing habit of referring to any measure put forward by the other fellows as a 'nostrum'. The word once meant a curative recipe or medicine, but it is a long time since anybody asked his chemist to give him a nostrum for catarrh. In politics a nostrum is always quackish and contemptible, which is absurd for a word meaning only 'our'. Surely if a measure is to be dismissed with disgust, the dismissing party should not thus appear to claim its ownership: 'a paltry vestrum' would make far better sense.

PLOY

WHILE lexicography relates the common 'employ', by way of the French, to the Latin *implicare*, the brief 'ploy' is set down as 'origin unknown'. Well, foundling or not, it is a good child, still flourishing north of Trent and Tweed for a hobby, occupation, adventure, or, when used of the mind, a fancy. So taken it is happily found in this quatrain of Mr. Macdiarmid's.

> Wheesht, wheesht, my foolish hert,
>   For weel ye ken
> I widna hae ye stert
>   Auld ploys again.

Ploys can be sinister. This I came across in Mr. Neil Gunn's tale of

North-East Scotland in the early nineteenth century, *The Silver Darlings*. Describing the licence of the old landowners, he writes,

> The minor lairds could, on occasion, exercise a lurid authority over a defenceless tenantry,

and he then talks of 'the shocking ploys' of these mean tyrants in relation to sexual matters.

Still, ugly as such ploys may have been, the word is attractive. Words are my personal ploy.

POW

THE dictionaries turn away from pow. Southern England will not acknowledge it. Burns made it familiar.

> But now your brow is bald, John,
>   Your locks are like the snow,
> But blessings on your frosty pow,
>   John Anderson, my Jo.

Again, of a limping and bent old man he wrote that he hirples

> Wi' his teethless gab and his auld beld pow.

But it is not just a Scotticism. In Mr. T. Thompson's robust and racy sketches and dialogues of Lancashire life there is often a gathering at the barber's. 'To pow' a man here is to cut his hair, and a nice, crisp term for it too. Pow-wow, for a putting of heads together in counsel and debate might come from this, but does not. It is one of the Red Man's gifts to his White conqueror. It is odd that, while the Redskin is usually pictured as a serene and silent chieftain, wrapped in tobacco-smoke and silence, one of our most graphic words for a talk should be his. Palaver, another good one, comes from Africa.

PRAGMATICAL

WORDS often go from good to worse: pragmatical has had one of these downhill slides. First it was practical: then busy; then over-busy. It has a good classical weight for the description of an interfering creature. With it Pepys truncheoned a too zealous constable encountered on a vinous and vagrant occasion.

> Home in a coach round by the wall; where we met so many stops by the watches, that it cost us much time and some trouble, and more money, to every watch to them to drink; this being encreased by the trouble the prentices did lately give the City, so that the militia and watches are very strict at this time; and we had like to have met with a stop for all night at the constable's watch at Mooregate by a pragmatical constable; but we came well home at about two in the morning.

Plainly, a difficult night. Wars and their permits and restrictions offer great chances to the busybody. The too pragmatical patriot is a common nuisance to his country.

PRIGGER

MUCH has been written about the richness of thieves' cant in Victorian times. There are, for example, such tributes to the nineteenth century lingo of the craft as Mr. W. L. Hanchant's *The Newgate Garland or Flowers of Hemp*, which is full of pretty terms. But for me the Tudor pamphleteers are supreme practitioners in description of the coney-catching tribe. Robert Greene, for example, could roll out a grand list of knavish nomenclature, with words as curt as they are expressive. 'And lastly look for a bead-roll or catalogue of all the names of the foists, nips, lifts, and priggers about London.' That quartette does indeed cram the town's rich thievery up. Fagin's world is here complete — and anticipated by two hundred and fifty years.

PUDGE

A PUDGE is a stout and puffy man. It is also a muddy puddle and good either way. John Clare liked pudge and the epithet pudgy, for his winter-landscapes. Among his Asylum Poems (this one so sanely observant and serene!) is,

> Little trotty wagtail, you nimble all about,
> And in the dimpling water-pudge you waddle in and out.

Nimble, as a verb, is nice.

PURSY

FROM quite old times pursy has been connected with the money-purse and meant purse-proud or wealthy. Also, because the strings of the purse are often drawn tight, it came to mean anything closely gathered: a pursy skin meant a tight, puckered covering for the face. But there is another pursy, a vigorous and expressive epithet, a corruption of pursive, meaning panting or broken-winded. Quarles sang of solitary folk in 'solemn groves'

> Where they sit and pant
> And breathe their pursy souls,
> Where neither grief consumes nor griping want
> Afflicts, nor sullen care controls.

I wonder whether Shakespeare may have had both senses in mind when he wrote, 'For in the fatness of these pursy times'.

The unfinancial, wheezing pursy is cousin to the French *poussif*. It reminds me of a drive in one of the antiquated landaus which survive in the Royal Deer Park, now public, at Klampenborg outside Copenhagen. (From this admirable piece of country motor-cars are excluded.) As we trotted agreeably along through the beech-groves a small boy with me asked the coachman what his horse's name was. 'Pouster' came the reply, that being the Danish for 'wheezer'. It might have been Pursy, which is really the same word and was a fairly accurate name in this case. Has poor Pouster become sausage-meat by now? If so, may he lie heavy on some pursy German's paunch.

PYRAMID

PYRAMIDS, more impressive by bulk than by design, bring a Greek name out of Egypt and, so doing, have appealed to the poets with most sense of an imposing sound. Milton deemed 'my Shakespeare's reliques' well enough famed without benefit of 'star-y pointing Pyramid', and Shakespeare himself had liked the word well. When

> palaces and pyramids do slope
> Their heads to their foundations

was Macbeth's idea of chaos come again. Cleopatra naturally mixed pyramids with her 'immortal longings'. Her defiance of the triumphant Augustus makes use of the four-syllabled plural which gave a rich roll to an iambic line.

> Shall they hoist me up,
> And show me to the shouting varletry
> Of censuring Rome? Rather a ditch in Egypt
> Be gentle grave unto me! rather on Nilus' mud
> Lay me stark nak'd, and let the water-flies
> Blow me into abhorring! rather make
> My country's high pyramides my gibbet,
> And hang me up in chains.

In our time the Pyramides have been a form of fireworks, which are often imaginatively titled toys (see my note on 'Tourbillion'), and the word has also denoted a variety of billiards. Furthermore it is also used for geometrical figures. But fie, as the Lady said in the Old Comedy, let us not be mathematical.

QUEASY

THIS is one of the fascinating words with an active and a passive meaning. It suggests both troublesome and troubled. The times, being queasy in fact, make men queasy of mind. A troubled mind may be the more exacting and so queasy comes to designate the fastidious. Probably its most frequent sense to-day is that of restlessness, inability to digest, gastric or mental tenderness. What helps to make it so expressive for us is its seeming collision of queer and uneasy. A queasy stomach is a phrase which proclaims itself. Queasy in Shakespeare may mean either disgusted ('queasy with his insolence'), fastidious, or sickly. Benedick had 'a quick wit and a queasy stomach'. With a transference of meaning from fastidious to feeble it can be most effectively given a slight turn of sneer. Those who in American slang 'are yellow and can't take it' are dismissible as queasy.

RANTIPOLE AND ROUSTABOUT

MR. OSBERT SITWELL, in the admirable book on Brighton, which he wrote with Miss Margaret Barton, quoted a ballad of 1815, signed 'Peter Pindar', called 'Royal Rantipoles, or The Humours of Brighton'. Rantipole implies a mixture of the romp and the rake, which suited the Regent well enough. 'Peter Pindar's' lyrical description of life at the Pavilion and of a royal game of 'Blind Man's Bluff', with the Prince laying hands upon the ladies, is distinctly rantipolitan.

It must be said of that age that its grossness was not in all things tyrannical. The Royal Rantipole had liberal impulses and gave freedom to burlesque: witness the licence which permitted the publication of this impudent Pindaric ode. Straying on so fine a word as roustabout one would naturally take it to be of the same family and reference as rantipole. Not at all. It is the American for a handyman. None the less, I suggest that 'Royal Roustabouts' would have been just as apt a name for 'Peter Pindar's' poem about the parlour-games of Prinny and his friends.

THERE is nearly always something rather likeably odd about the words ending in double 'e'. One feels that a raree-show must be a good one, its rareties genuinely scarce, its freaks freakish beyond a peradventure, and its showmanship terrific. Grandees came from Castile and there was no doubt about their grandeur, just as there can be no second thoughts about the viciousness of a debauchee. Raree, like debauchee, has become too rare nowadays. Of rare Ben Jonson it could be added that his masques and plays present a double raree-show, one of fantastic characters and humours, the other of the English language. A later type of notable exhibition was the galanty-show or shadow-pantomime. The term is too rich a one to be limited to so jejune a matter as shadow-play and silhouette. All the history of fops and pretenders, of bucks and macaronis and possibly of genuine heroes too, is surely a galanty-show.

RATHE

I HAVE seen 'rathe' dismissed as obsolete. It is a calamity, if it be so. For it is a strong and simple word for all speedy and vehement things.

> I am the hunte which rathe and early ryse.

Then it acquired a special reference to flowers and fruits which are lured on by early sun and gallantly, perhaps rashly, anticipate their hour, like Milton's 'rathe primrose'. It is odd that Shakespeare, with his grand sweep of vocabulary, should have missed 'rathe'. It was perfect for his daffodils that 'come before the swallow dares'.

REAM

IN the note on Nappy the word 'reaming' occurred. It is Scottish and northern and much happier, with its creamy suggestion, than the meagre frothy. Drinking songs tend to be monotonous and boring. Eulogies of beer, after we have flavoured such old favourites as 'Bring us in good ale' and 'Back and sides go bare', become rather tedious. The best descriptions of beer come from the land of whisky. Alexander Hume, for example (1557-1602), in his sun-drenched poem 'Of the Day Estivall', deals thus with Scotland's summer-thirst:

> The Caller wine in cave is sought,
>   Men's brothing breasts to cool;
> The water cauld and clear is brought,
>   And sallets steept in ule.
> Some plucks the honey-plum and pear,
>   The cherry and the pêche:
> Some likes the reamand London beer
>   The body to refresh.

London beer, presumably, was a Trade Title. It is hardly to be supposed that sixteenth-century Scotland took London's liquor on so long a journey. Robert Fergusson in 'The Farmer's Ingle', on which Burns drew closely for 'The Cotter's Saturday Night', writes:

> O' nappy liquor owre a bleezin' fire:
>   Sair wark and poortith downa weel be joined;
> Wi' butter'd bannocks now the girdle reeks,
>   I' the far nook the bowie briskly reams.

Poortith is poverty, the bowie a bowl or tub. Sair work and poortith have not yet been disjoined. But the nappy and 'the swats' still ream for consolation.

RENEGE

RENEGE means to desert, or renounce. Sometimes it is spelt reneague. It was a Tudor word, used of religious recantation and still surviving apparently in the Scottish slang of crooks, for so James Bridie, the dramatist, has employed it in his dialogue. I was surprised and glad to find it there, for I thought this nicely descriptive word had not been much heard since Shakespeare said of the love-shackled Antony,

> his captain's heart,
> Which in the scuffles of great fights hath burst
> The buckles on his breast, reneges all temper,
> And is become the bellows and the fan
> To cool a gipsy's lust.

Lear's Kent has it too in his railing at the varlet Oswald, whom he groups with the smiling rogues who

> Renege, affirm, and turn their halcyon beaks
> With every gale and vary of their masters,
> Knowing naught, like dogs, but following.

Halcyon beaks is exciting and halcyon has already been put in the honours list. Mr. Arthur Ransome tells me of a boatman at Barrow who bade him not renege, i.e. abandon an audacious plan of navigation.

RUBIOUS

THE ruby has ceased to be a fashionable gem and Ruby as a Christian name is now rare. But the word has the richness which the letter 'R' so often confers, as Fitzgerald was well aware.

> But still the Vine her ancient Ruby yields.

The second noun does powerfully suggest a splendour on the palate and a glow in the mind. All who have ever lost their heart to Shakespeare's Viola — that is all who ever read *Twelfth Night* — remember the delicate cherry of her mouth,

> Diana's lip
> Is not more smooth and rubious.

The jewel has here turned gentle and this 'rubious' seems very far removed from the crude scarlet slash favoured in the make-up of so many a contemporary miss.

RUSSET is one of those words which may be described as happily telescoped or double-barrelled. It meant reddish-brown, and could be handsomely employed so. To talk of 'The dawn in russet mantle clad' was to pay a compliment, but the 'rus' element evidently suggested rusticity and plainness, so that russet's red was turned to a plebeian rustiness. At length it could be used without much notion of colour at all, but simply to imply an honest simplicity. Oliver Cromwell employed it thus of his captains, russet-coated men, as opposed to the foppish Cavaliers. Biron in *Love's Labour's Lost*, that spruce courtier of a too inventive tongue, when corrected, promised to abandon

> Taffeta phrases, silken terms precise

and to go a-wooing,

> In russet yeas and honest kersey noes.

There is a particularly nice use of russet in Thomas Fuller's picture of the Good English Yeoman.

> He wears russet clothes, but makes golden payment, having tin in his buttons, and silver in his pocket. If he chance to appear in clothes above his rank, it is to grace some great man with his service, and then he blusheth at his own bravery. Otherwise he is the surest landmark, whence foreigners may take aim of the ancient English customs; the gentry more floating after foreign fashions.

Emily Dickinson proclaimed it 'an honourable thought'

> That we've immortal place,
> Though pyramids decay,
> And kingdoms, like the orchard,
> Flit russetly away.

We might ourselves now flit or float, in Fuller's phrase, after home-products and keep the good russet in our speech as well as in our apple-trees.

SANGUINE

SANGUINE has sometimes meant bloody or bloodthirsty, but its usual modern meaning is gentler. To the medieval doctor there were four 'complexions' of the human system, sanguine being that in which blood was predominant. Hence sanguine folk were ruddy, confident, brave, and amorous at their youthful best and, at their latter and less charming end, apoplectic. According to Thomas Tryon, described by Mr. Jan Gordon as a seventeenth-century 'Pythagorean, vegetarian, teetotaller, feminist, and educator' (an astonishing mixture for that period)

> Oxen are dignified with a Sanguine, Melancholick Nature a little inclined to the Phlegmatick. Sheep are Sanguine and Phlegmatick with a little mixture of Melancholly. . . .

The distinctions are nice, but a trifle subtle for the farm-yard. Tryon adds that Swine are 'Melancholly and Cholerick' only, which at first seems complete nonsense to anybody who has pondered over pigsties. Surely, you would say, a litter of brisk young porkers is the very essence of sanguinity. But choler, to the Elizabethan, was, in Bacon's words, 'an humour that maketh men active, earnest, full of alacrity, and stirring'. So let us pass the choleric pig. But melancholy? Never.

SARABAND

DANCING in our time has reached the muddy depths of nomenclature, making its jerky and cacophonous progress from the Bunny Hug to the Black Bottom. We still import our jitterbugs and heeby-jeebies: boogie-woogie has presumably come in with 'bands across the sea'. We have had our democratic folk-dances from jig and morris to Valeta and Lambeth Walk. But we always have imported for courtly elegance. There was, however, this difference, that in the old days our importations had grace of sound as well as of motion. Shakespeare's London moved from a berga-

mask to 'heel the high lavolt' (Italians both), and thence to the
Spanish saraband, which, whatever its optical charms, is also a
glorious noise. Bottom offered Theseus an epilogue or a bergamask
after the play of Pyramus and Thisbe, but both were prudently
declined. The English saraband was born in the year of Shakespeare's death.

> And the strains of the sarabande
> More lively than a madrigal,
> Go hand in hand
> Like the river and its waterfall,

sings Mr. Sacheverell Sitwell of public dancings by the Rio
Grande. So once in Whitehall the lordly masquers of the Stuart
court trod this euphonious measure.

SCAMBLE

WHY on earth has this excellent and convenient verb been allowed
to sink into the dictionary's 'Obs. and Arch.', the graveyard, so often,
of the just? Scamble seems to have been all things to all men. By
scambling money you squandered it. Or by scambling money up
you hoarded money up. To scamble a meal was the same as our
'knocking up' and a scambler was the visitor whom you had to
oblige with this process, often so much more laborious than one
expects. A scambler is a really good word for the person who looks
in a little before supper. To scamble was also to wander or lounge
and so to be a kind of strolling wastrel and knave. Antonio, of
Much Ado About Nothing, uses it in an angry dismissal of smart,
swaggering knaves:

> What, man! I know them, yea,
> And what they weigh, even to the utmost scruple —
> Scambling, out-facing, fashion-mongering boys,
> That lie and cog and flout, deprave and slander . . .

From this the passage is obvious to the fine dismissive phrase for
mental vapouring, 'skimble-skamble stuff'.

SCRUNTY

SCRUNTY is Scottish and you can form your own idea of what it means simply by looking at it and muttering the two syllables. It occurs in the tale of bad Robin-a-Ree, a ballad admired and quoted by Charlotte Brontë's Caroline Helstone.

> Oh! ance I lived happily by yon bonny burn —
>   The warld was in love wi' me;
> But now I maun sit 'neath the cauld drift and mourn
>   And curse black Robin-a-Ree!
>
> Then whudder awa', thou bitter biting blast,
>   And sough through the scrunty tree,
> And smoor me up in the snaw fu' fast,
>   And ne'er let the sun me see!

Whudder, sough, scrunty and smoor, all in three lines! The Scots have rarely been great artists in music, but as ballad-makers they were immense and in the making of words they showed a rare genius for the look and the cadence and the flavour of the thing, be it bonnie and blithe or scrunty merely.

SECRETARY

HOW often does the user of the word secretarial think of it in terms of deep confidence? Indeed, the fact that we have to employ the phrase 'confidential secretary' shows how far the original meaning has disappeared. (Really, one might as well talk about a culinary cook.) The Secretary of State was the man who held the secrets of the nation and any secretary's first business was rather to keep his mouth shut and ears open than to write and file letters. Hence secretary was applied to any conniver at privacies, especially to darkness. In an anonymous seventeenth century poem of passion, drawing obviously on Latin sources, I came across the word in that connection.

Let us begin while daylight springs in heaven
And kiss till night descends into the even,
And when that modest secretary, night,
Discovers all but thy heaven-beaming light
We will begin revels of hidden love
In that sweet orb where silent pleasures move.

Shakespeare only uses secretary in its modern, official sense, perhaps because he already had so many exquisite metaphors for night's concealment.

SEEL AND SEELY

EVERYBODY knows Macbeth's invitation to the dark.

> Come seeling night,
> Scarf up the tender eye of pitiful day.

Most people probably take seeling to be a Tudor spelling of sealing. But it is a different verb, derived, like many Tudor terms, from falconry. Seeling was a part of the taming and training process and meant tying up the birds' eyelids with a thread. So Antony employed the metaphor.

> But when we in our viciousness grow hard —
> Oh misery on't — the wise gods seel our eyes:
> In our own filth drop our clear judgments: make us
> Adore our errors: laugh at us, while we strut
> To our confusion.

Seely is an odd word: it has nothing to do with the falconer's seeling, but is not quite the same as silly, since it first meant well-omened and lucky. Then, by way of piety, it came to imply simplicity and so to be united with silly, of which more in its proper place. Ben Jonson in his verses in the Shakespearean First Folio wrote of 'Seeliest ignorance'. He probably meant simple and had no thought of the verb seel and its darkness.

H   113

SILLY has become a term of contempt, but to the men of Shakespeare's time it implied an honourable form of simplicity. 'Like to the seely fly, to the dear light I fly', sang Davison. The poets of that epoch habitually contrasted the uneasy glory of a courtier's life with the homespun safety of the peasant's cot. When Campion warned the 'courtly dames and knights' that

> Yet, for all your pomp and train,
> Securer lives the silly swain,

he was not deeming his Jack and Joan to be fools. The meaning had not changed when Burns wrote of the silly walls of the field-mouse's nest. Shakespeare also used silly in this sense and it was applied to sheep to describe their innocence rather than their lack of brain. In the beautiful passage in *Henry VI*, Part III, where the young King Henry muses on the happier life of the 'homely swain', a passage manifestly prophetic of the superb monologues of *Richard II*, the King exclaims,

> Ah, what a life were this! how sweet! how lovely!
> Gives not the hawthorn-bush a sweeter shade
> To shepherds, looking on their silly sheep,
> Than doth a rich embroider'd canopy
> To kings that fear their subjects' treachery?
> O, yes, it doth; a thousand-fold it doth.
> And to conclude, — the shepherd's homely curds,
> His cold thin drink out of his leather bottle,
> His wonted sleep under a fresh tree's shade,
> All which secure and sweetly he enjoys,
> Is far beyond a prince's delicates,
> His viands sparkling in a golden cup,
> His body couched in a curious bed,
> When care, mistrust, and treason wait on him.

The whole passage is worth citing in a note of this kind because of its further and nice usage of delicates and curious.

SMIRK

SMIRK is a good old word for neat and trim, cousin to smikker which is a casualty in England but still, in a similar form, is the ordinary word for pretty in Denmark. We can hardly now dissociate smirk from a knowing, leering glance and to find a 'Smirk Butler' in Herrick is no doubt particularly pleasing because of its hint of a Davus, even of a Jeeves. The Smirk Butler appears in the parson's robustly sensuous Nuptiall Song or Epithalamie on Sir Clipseby Crew and his lady ('To bed, to bed, kind Turtles') and is described as eager to express his wit in the arrangement of napery and even as striving to catch her ladyship's eye. I have a feeling that Sir Clipseby may have found it necessary to be rid of the fellow before long and to find a rather less smirk successor. What did Herrick mean exactly by 'smirking wine'? Smiling, bubbling? Here is the passage.

> If smirking wine be wanting here,
> There's that which drowns all care, stout beere.

Wycherley used smirk with the odious sense that we attach to it, attributing to one of his characters 'the canonical smirk and filthy clammy palm of a chaplain'.

SNIDE AND SNOOP

THESE two words are mainly used in America and deserve to go on the list of England's necessary imports. Snide for bogus or dishonest has some record of English usage, but it is far commoner in America, where it is a living and expressive term. I have noticed it several times in the works of Mr. George Jean Nathan, who is not as a rule addicted to archaism. His 'snide lawyers' are just the men to employ some snooping creatures. Snoop, of a Dutch origin, is a superb word for poking and prying and hiding and spying. Like snide, it seems only to have visited England. Both migrants should be henceforth impounded and naturalized.

SOCIAL

POOR social! It has fallen on bleak times and now is almost invariably tagged to a 'problem' or a 'service'. This friendly and liquorish word has become Blue Bookish and as dry as a Report on Stitchery Instruction in Girls' Clubs. Moreover, the older and happier meaning has also been applied to such oppressive occasions. 'A social evening', 'A social function'. Does any heart beat at the phrase, does any eye sparkle? What would Burns have made of these celebrations? Yet social was a great word of his, as of his century, and was usually applied to the happiest of moods and of refreshments.

> So may through Albion's farthest ken
>   To social flowing glasses
> The grace be 'Athole's honest men
>   And Athole's bonnie lasses'.

In the Epistle to James Smith, with its defence of 'the hairum-scarum, ram-stam boys, The rattling squad', there is ample praise of 'Cheerfu' tankards foamin' And social noise'.

The social cup should come again to ease our weariness with social problems.

SPANIEL

THE use of 'spaniel' as a verb is typical of Shakespeare's flash of phrase. With what a prodigal collision of metaphors does he describe the desertion of Antony that followed the treachery of Cleopatra! First he cries out that she

> Like a right gipsy hath at fast and loose
> Beguiled me to the very heart of loss.

Then he adds,

>   The hearts
> That spaniel'd me at heels, to whom I gave
> Their wishes, do discandy, melt their sweets
> On blossoming Caesar and this pine is barked
> That overtopped them all.

Spaniels are the only dogs about which Shakespeare is frequently particular. The hounds in general he knows, the 'shoughs, water-rugs, and demi-wolves' and, of course, the mastiffs of the baiting-pit and bull-ring, his theatre's neighbours at Paris Garden. But of terriers he says nothing. Spaniel he employs as noun, adjective, and verb, making it the symbol of affectionate humility. His spaniel is sometimes seen as basely fawning, perhaps, but also as the happy and likeable tail-wagger. I surmise a genial grovelling of spaniels at New Place and one of this species as the earliest Bardolater or worshipper of Mr. W. S. The verb is delightful, and I am happy, here as ever, to spaniel on Shakespeare's use of words.

SQUANDER

OUR limiting of squander to financial matters has narrowed the usage of a vivid word. Squander was first an intransitive verb and meant to be scattered. Flocks squandered. Then it became more active and meant to disperse. When Shylock calls Antonio's argosies 'squandered abroad' he means locally dispersed and is not thinking of monetary wastage. So with Jaques.

> The wise man's folly is anatomized
> Even by the squandering glances of the fool.

Edmund Blunden, whose use of words is always fascinating, employs squander with aptness in his beautiful poem 'The Alms-women'.
With

> At Quincey's moat the squandering village ends,

he begins his picture of the old village women:

> All things they have in common, being so poor,
> And this one fear, Death's shadow, at the door.
> Each sundown makes them mournful, each sunrise
> Brings back the brightness in their failing eyes.

Squandering is so exactly right for the end of an English village as it fades off into its little chaos of orchards and of cabbage-patch, of shippons and tool-sheds and tumble-down steadings of all kind.

STADDLE

A SERVICEABLE old word for a support or crutch or a staff of any kind. If you grow weary of reading about 'Pillars of Society', it is because we have forgotten our Staddles of the State. Mr. Churchill proved himself at the dangerous hour to be every inch a Staddle. The word is metaphorically taken from forestry in which a staddle is a tree left standing when others are thinned out. Thomas Fuller, discussing the means of raising good infantry as well as wealthy cavaliers, wrote,

> Wherefore, to make good infantry, it requireth men bred, not in a servile or indigent fashion, but in some free and plentiful manner. Wisely, therefore, did that knowing prince, King Henry the Seventh, provide laws for the increase of his yeomanry, that his kingdom should not be like to coppice-woods, where, the staddles being left too thick, all runs to bushes and briers, and there is little clean underwood.

The word's usage has dwindled, but the doctrine holds.

STALWART

EARLIER I mentioned the politicians' delight in cliché. The British parties have developed their inseparable adjectives. The old and bold of Liberalism are always described as 'Stalwarts', while Tories are always Stout. Labour favours Staunch.

Stalwart is my favourite of these. It is, in fact, a form of the older, 'stalworth', which means worthy of a place or seat and is thus an excellent word for a politician. (Stalwart accordingly is really equivalent to the phrase 'A representative man', which helped to carry Mr. Veneering into Parliament for the Borough of Pocket

Breaches, with his friends enthusiastically 'rallying round' and with that incomparable duo of toadies, Messrs. Boots and Brewer, told to 'take cabs and go about' as the very essence of the rallying process.) But nowadays 'stalwart' has a strong hint of chesty, 'chin-up' men who never doubt that clouds will break. I can clearly visualize a 'Liberal Stalwart' or a 'Stout Tory'. The staunch Labourite remains cloudier. Why, by the way, do many of our terms for endurance begin with 'st'? Not only are men of stamina stalwart, stout, and staunch, but they are strong, stubborn, strenuous, sturdy, and steadfast stickers-to-the-end.

STOLCHY

STOLCHY, meaning trampled into mire, I found in Edmund Blunden, Suffolk's singer and the worthy editor of John Clare, both being bards so earthy and ethereal at once.

> When groping farms are lanterned up
> And stolchy ploughlands hid in grief,
> And glimmering by-roads catch the drop
> That weeps from sprawling twig and leaf . . .

This, I take it the East Anglian, form of the word is much better than the more general 'stoach' and 'stoachy'. Kipling wrote of fields 'stoached with sliding hoof-marks'. But the 'l' is sovereign. It powerfully stiffens the mire and expresses all the squelch and struggle of a walk across November clay.

When I once used the word 'stolchy' a correspondent reminded me of the Scottish and Northern English 'clarty' which appears to mean much the same thing. But clarty, to me, has a clear, sharp, frosty tang, which is very different. Clarty would be a grand word for a day of sun, rime, and east wind.

STOUR

THE English have kept the finely-sounding stour only for their rivers. Otherwise it has been left to the Scots. It meant battle and also any sort of struggle or stress: from that it came to denote tumult and the dust of combat. Altogether it is a nicely expressive word, effectively used by Spenser for whom it was English enough, but then relegated to the North where it abides in what is left of Scots. It has the deep note of doom and is a grand word for a stern occasion, as Dunbar knew well. In his *Lament for the Makars* he says of the 'tyrand' Death,

> He takis the campion[1] in the stour,
> The captain closit in the tour,
> The lady in bour full of bewtie:

And Burns, in one of his most memorable songs, cried from the heart,

> How blithely wad I bide the stoure,
> A weary slave frae sun to sun,
> Could I the rich reward secure,
> The lovely Mary Morison.

How mean the English 'stir' seems after that! Scottish realism has used the dusty side of it with effect. John Muir, the grave-digger in *Cloud Howe*, Lewis Grassic Gibbon's wonderful study of small-town life in the Mearns, talks of mankind going down to 'stour and stink' in the end.

THRILL

JOURNALISM, as I have already noted, seizes on the short word, seizes and soon works it to death. 'Thrill' has been one of its most unhappy victims. Originally it meant a shiver down the back and the adjective thrilling was applied to things shiversome on the grand scale. In Shakespeare thrill is tremendous. 'I have a faint cold fear thrills through my veins.' We should shudder at that. In Claudio's magnificent speech on the terrors of death thrilling, now tagged to any tawdry event or stage-surprise, magnificently takes its place.

[1] Champion.

Ay, but to die, and go we know not where;
To lie in cold obstruction, and to rot;
This sensible warm motion to become
A kneaded clod; and the delighted spirit
To bathe in fiery floods or to reside
In thrilling regions of thick-ribbed ice,
To be imprison'd in the viewless winds,
And blown with restless violence round about
The pendent world;

Thrilling there comes in like a whip-lash of East wind — or did to an Elizabethan. When Charlotte Brontë wrote of 'thrilling pains in her back' she meant agony. Thrilling has retained its dignity and power in some modern poetry. In Kipling's Sussex,

Here through the strong and shadeless days
The tinkling silence thrills.

This splendidly mingles the sheep-bells and the stab of sun upon the treeless chalk. In Laurence Binyon's famous poem 'For the Fallen'

Solemn the drums thrill: Death, august and royal,
Sings sorrow up into immortal spheres.

But the 'boosters' of the Entertainment Industry, as well as the hard-pressed sub-editors seeking a short word for excitement, have effectively murdered thrill by now and are pathetically striving to revive it with emphatic prefix. I recently read a puff of a film with 'A Thousand Super-Thrills'. As if that helped!

TOPIARY

THE topiary art is that of trimming hedges and bushes into fantastic shape. The Tudor gardeners were topiarists of distinction and one would expect the eighteenth century to have enjoyed the formalities of the craft. But Addison and Pope denounced topiary in gardens, Pope announcing heavily that 'all art consists in the imitation and study of nature', which seems to be a sweeping misstatement. Pope went on to quote (or invent) ludicrously from the catalogues of topiary in his time.

> Adam and Eve in Yew. Adam a little shattered by the fall of the tree of knowledge in the great storm: Eve and the Serpent very flourishing,

and

> Divers eminent modern poets, in bays, somewhat blighted, to be disposed of, a pennyworth.

The truth surely is that topiary in gardens suits houses and estates of a certain period. Round a great Tudor mansion the peacock should stand in yew as well as strutting in full feather.

TOSY

TOSY and cosh both mean snug and are very happily used by John Galt in his *Annals of the Parish*. His Rev. Mr. Balwhidder complains of the tea-drinking that has come unto Ayrshire (1762), but reminds himself that it does less harm than the 'Conek' (cognac) with which previous beverages had been laced.

> There is no meeting now in the summer evenings, as I remember often happened in my younger days, with decent ladies coming home with red faces, tosy and cosh, from a posset-masking.

Could there be better adjectives to suggest a modest alcoholic after-glow? One thinks of the 'decent ladies' very affable with the Minister and then reduced to tittering and even to less than decent conversation when Mr. Balwhidder had passed by.

Cosh, by the way, was the name of one of John Aubrey's sources of information. That glorious gossip, after relating some neat or scandalous episode, would note, 'This I had of old Major Cosh'. The Major suggests one of the ripest of the seventeenth-century talkers. He was doubtless almost always tosy.

TOURBILLION

ANYTHING which goes round and round, especially a firework which gyrates. A good word, surely, for the literary or dramatic critic. Is not Bernard Shaw the unquenchable tourbillion of the theatre, is not H. G. Wells the restless tourbillion of the Left? G. K. Chesterton was certainly the gyrating firework of the Faith, the Catherine Wheel of orthodoxy, in his day. The old descriptions of firework displays are always delightful. When Stratford-on-Avon celebrated the birthday of Shakespeare in 1830, a Mr. Robert Southby, of the Royal Gardens, Vauxhall, London, did his best to set the Avon on fire with his unparalleled array of 'Pyramids, Batteries, Saucissons, Mines, and Tourbillions'. So let us have fewer stale metaphors from the hard-worked rocket and some fresh ones from these glories of a nineteenth-century nocturne, the tourbillion especially.

TOURMALINE

THIS substance, which sounds like something sensual in Swinburne, is, in fact, 'a brittle pyro-electric mineral' and 'a complex silicoborate with a vitreous lustre': also 'a specimen or gem of this mineral'. Why then include it in a book of estimable words? Because it is the kind of jewel that used to flash in the vocabulary of aspiring poets and is doing so again. It occurs along with agate, sphene, jacinth, topaz, sardonyx, and feldspar, in a poem on Euterpe by a very young and rather mineralogical minstrel, Mr. A. G. Lambert, who shared a volume called *Silver Gold* with his colleague, Mr. A. J. Neame, while both were attending Cheltenham College.[1] The latter bard was as much excited by Echo as Mr. Lambert was by Euterpe.

> Her tiara is garnet and bright tourmaline,
> With glittering facets of chrysoberyl light.

[1] Cheltenham's previous output of minstrels was limited to Adam Lindsay Gordon, a vigorous Australian rhymer with a strong equestrian interest. Mr. Day Lewis was for a while, I believe, a master in the Junior School.

For some years the English Muse has been robbed of these sonorous and romantic gems and decorated with the metaphor of fuse-box and flash-point, algebra and internal combustion engines. Here is some rescue of poetry from petrol and power-stations. Once more the English Muse may have rings on her fingers and bells on her toes and tourmaline may decorate both.

TRAFFIC

TRAFFIC, like horde previously noted, is a dog with a bad name. Why should it always be applied, in its trading sense, to shameful practices or articles deemed to be sinister and degrading? It was not always so. When Shakespeare talked of 'the two hours traffic of our stage' he was not implying dirty fun or censorable themes. Michael Drayton, honouring Shakespeare, claimed for him the ownership of

> As strong conception and as cleere a rage
> As any one that trafiqu'd with the stage.

(A clear rage is surely a most striking phrase for the kind of genius who, like Shakespeare, can lose his heart in his work and also keep his head.) But nowadays traffic is the word always chosen by the man who would abuse and even prohibit his neighbour's profession. To the fanatical teetotaller there is no such thing as 'having a glass of beer', which many citizens innocently imagine themselves to be doing. No, they are 'partaking of alcoholic stimulants purveyed by the Liquor Traffic'. This talk of the Liquor Traffic — monstrous phrase which includes the rarest claret with the roughest bath-tub gin — puts wine on a level with cocaine. Drugs, of course, are always the matter of a Traffic. I should like to rescue poor Traffic and reinstate it in good repute. Why not talk of the rose-traffic in Covent Garden or of the traffic in Holy Writ carried on by the British and Foreign Bible Society?

TREPAN

TREPAN now chiefly signifies a surgical instrument for cutting out pieces of bone, especially from the skull, and the act of so cutting. But to our ancestors it was a snare and the user of a snare and a very forcible word it was. Seventeenth and eighteenth century invective is resonant with 'Rogues and Trepans'. I have advocated the renewal of the word 'Cog' for cheating and cozening and with it I would have trepan. Burns applied it to the gay seducer in 'The Jolly Beggars',

> The ladies' hearts he did trepan
> My gallant, braw John Highlandman.

The surgeons must not have so good a thing to themselves.

UMBER

ALL through winter Britain abounds in exquisite tints. Blake's 'green and pleasant land' has become brown and russet. The bare, ruin'd choirs have their sombre splendour of tint as well as of form. But the writer who endeavours to paint this glory in words finds himself with a galling scarcity of satisfactory epithets of colour. Dun is a dull word and sepia smacks of the paint-box rather than of the vivid beauty of woods in winter. I have a liking for umber, which may or may not be connected with the Latin word for shade. That connection has long been lost: to Shakespeare umber was a pigment for staining things and disguising the complexion. ('And with a kind of umber smirch my face.') Now it has come to signify brown in general and its depth of sound suggests a like depth of colour-tone. For Housman,

> Wenlock Edge was umbered
> And bright was Abdon Burf
> And warm between them slumbered
> The smooth green miles of turf.

The adjective not only delights the ear: it helps to drench the stanza with the more sombre pigments of our coloured counties. Umber, I am told, is one name for a grayling, which by its swift, underwater movement acquires the dark look of a shadow.

UMBRAGE

Why not restore to umbrage its proper meaning of shadow? Now it seems always to bear its later sense of disfavour and, there too, it is in disfavour, or at least in mockery. Who talks of 'taking umbrage' except as a joke? But umbrage, in its true significance, is a good, black, shadowy term for suggesting a dense covering of leafy or needled branches.

Milton's

> When highest woods impenetrable
> To star or sunlight spread their umbrage broad

drives into the dark heart of silvan gloom. Hamlet used umbrage for the shadow of a man and any word in Hamlet's vocabulary has a prescriptive right to endurance. For adjectives there are umbratile and umbrageous, umbrous and umbrose. Umbrageous is the most common. Carlyle's Teufelsdrockh, that ingenious and impassioned spinner of words, moved on 'umbrageous lawns'. Umbratile will not do now. It too unhappily suggests the pert trade name of a patent waterproof hat. Umbrageous might also be a telescoping of umbrage with outrageous and is not right for quiet, shady places. Umbrose hints at a man called Ambrose in a pet. Umbrous is best. Meanwhile we have to recover umbrage from its status of a slightly comic alternative to 'dudgeon' and put it back among green thoughts beneath the trees.

UNCONSCIONABLE

In the note on 'barkable' allusion was made to the various employments of the termination -able. Unconscionable is an example of the oddest use. It is the equivalent of unconscientious. Why it took its present form is difficult to see. Does it mean something that conscience cannot cope with, or is it simply the fine, dismissive sound which has shaped it thus queerly? The eighteenth century drama is full of unconscionable dogs and rogues, for the epithet comes soundingly upon the angry lips of Sir Olivers and Sir Anthonys. From unconscientious it came to mean perverse or preposterous or extreme, as in the familiar royal apology for being 'an unconscionable time a-dying'. And most effective it is there.

VALE

A COMMON word, indeed, for I am not thinking of the bisyllabic 'vale', Latin for farewell, beautiful as that is too. How much more appropriate to its object is the now rather poetic vale than the usual valley! For vale is broad and flowing like the northern dale, while valley is a mean, scampering little word. Wordsworth, who was much less of a mountaineer than of a dalesman, made constant melody of dale and vale, far more than of fell and ghyll. He loved their feeling of expanse with gentleness. The Highlanders have permitted one Lake (instead of Loch) and one Vale (instead of Strath, glen being reserved for the steep and narrow defiles). The single Highland Vale is that of Atholl, down whose broad loveliness the Tummell gallops to meet the Tay. Strath Atholl would have been difficult and ugly. So the Highlanders wisely accepted the English Vale and the Vale of Atholl remains the perfect name for the green and tranquil levels between the surge of Grampians East and West.

VENUST

I HAVE never thought that the Latin word Venus, whether pronounced in the English manner or as Waynoose, was musically adequate to its subject. Yet the old adjective 'venust', used by the Scots makars, has always pleased me. How did they pronounce it? 'Venoust', I suppose, in which case it becomes a pretty addition to the language of love. The Latinism of the Scots poets of the latter part of the sixteenth century, so magnificent in the use of their native words, is sometimes oppressive. Is 'The Day Estivall', as Hume called it, preferable to 'The Summer Day'? But when a lover woos his

> tender babe venust

one immediately accepts her as adorable and regrets that the English dictionaries now pass the word by. Alexander Scott's use of it occurs in the lovely as well as alliterative verse,

> My bird, bonnie ane,
>> My tender babe venust,
> My luve, my life alane,
>> My liking and my lust.

Certainly this poem is a frank one, but not heavily so. The word lust, now possessing an ugly as well as an adipose tissue, has put on weight with the years, and to Scott was far closer to the German notion of a 'lustig' or merry state of mind.

WAG

WHILE staying with a farmer-friend in the Oxfordshire Cotswolds I asked him about local dialect words. He told me that Old Tom, his labourer, called his son his 'wag'. Wag, for a boy, with no implication of facetiousness, is Tudor English. Thomas Fuller wrote that 'Queen Elizabeth, coming into a Grammar School, made this extemporary verse,

> 'Persius a Crab-staffe, Bawdy Martial,
>> Ovid a fine Wag'.

It now seems less than brilliant. By wag the Queen meant not a jester, but a brisk, gay fellow. When Shakespearean characters call each other 'Good wag' or 'Sweet wag' they are not necessarily implying that the youngster is an intending comedian. Imogen, when going into breeches, is advised by Pisanio to 'change her niceness into a waggish courage', i.e. the courage of a lad. But the idea of playfulness has begun to break in.

>As waggish boys in game themselves forswear

says Helena. The modern notion of a wag, as a fellow of any age who eternally strives after quips and puns, is quite different. Old Tom when he calls his son 'my wag' may mean that his lad is a lively one, but does not wish to suggest word-play and facetiousness. Incidentally, Tom lives within twenty miles of Stratford-on-Avon. Robert Burns employed 'wag' for the 'bad lad' of the village, as we say. These lines must have been noted in Ayrshire at the time and are not forgotten now.

> Lament him, Mauchline husbands a',
>   He often did assist ye;
> For had ye staid whole weeks awa',
>   Your wives they ne'er had missed ye.

> Ye Mauchline bairns, as on ye pass
>   To school in bands the gither,
> O, tread ye lightly on his grass,
>   Perhaps he was your father.

They are headed 'Epitaph on a Wag in Mauchline'.

Garrick, in writing one of his Shakespearean odes, spoke of his hero as the 'Warwickshire wag'. For him it was equivalent to lad.

WAMBLE AND WIMPLE

THERE are many vivid words for unsteady things beginning with 'w'. What more vivid than 'a wambling stomach', for a disturbed one? Pistol's paunch must have wambled much 'when qualmy at the smell of leak'. All shaky, tottering things, from the stomach to the State, have been effectively criticized as wambling. Wimple, as a verb (not as the noun which denotes a copious form of head-dress) is a gentler term and means to meander. That last word, itself an aptly sounding one, comes from the river Meander in Asia Minor. Wimple is mainly Scottish. Burns loved 'a wimpling burn' and so might anybody.

WAN

DIM has been given inclusion. Shall wan remain behind? A beautiful word for all pale, lack-lustre things, it throws a shadow wherever it strikes. What better entry than that first line of King Henry IV, now wearing the murdered Richard's crown?

> So shaken as we are, so wan with care,

But, apart from the everlastingly wan stars of romance and the wan maids more lovesick than any of Castle Bunthorne, my chief reason for bringing in this frail monosyllable is desire to cite the exquisite use of it in the Scottish ballad of Fair Annie, which begins with what is surely the cruellest stanza in all such doleful story.

> It's narrow, narrow, mak your bed,
>   And learn to lie your lane;
> For I'm gaun owre the sea, Fair Annie,
>   A braw bride to bring hame.
> Wi' her I will get gowd and gear,
>   Wi' you I ne'er gat nane.

When the 'braw bride' was brought in:

> Fair Annie served the lang tables
>   Wi' the white bread and the wine;
> But ay she drank the wan water
>   To keep her colour fine.

The wan water! There is a splash of magic in that. The impact is physical and unforgettable.

WANDER

WANDER is a simple and a common word, one of those whose beauty and expressiveness are overlooked just because of their familiarity. But say it to yourself as though you had never seen or heard of it before. It has far more of loneliness and bewilderment in the sound of it than have our Latin words for the same thing, errant or vagrant or even vagabond. (This last is the best of the three.) What an exquisite line is Wordsworth's

> I wandered lonely as a cloud.

No 'staying in solitude' could approach its emotional tone. The sound of wandering to me suggests enormous spaces and cold, unfeeling vacancies, perhaps because it occurs so majestically in those amazing lines in the Epistle of St. Jude in which certain ungodly and lascivious men are withered with a ferocity of cold damnation as relentless as a night of Russian winter.

> These are the spots in your feasts of charity, when they feast with you, feeding themselves without fear: clouds they are, without water, carried about of winds: trees whose fruit withereth, without fruits, twice dead, plucked up by the roots: raging waves of the sea, foaming out their own shame: wandering stars, to whom is reserved the blackness of darkness for ever.

Incomparable climax with its trisyllabic trinity, 'the blackness of darkness for ever'! War-time nights taught us the full menace of that unrelenting phrase. But the chill of 'wandering stars' had previously done its work.

WATCHET

WATCHET, for several tints of blue, is dismissed by the dictionaries as 'Obs. or arch.'. But Lamb used it of the uniforms worn by the boys in Christ's Hospital and it came naturally to John Clare, who did not die till 1862.

> But now the evening curdles dank and gray,
> Changing her watchet hue for sombre weed;
> And moping owls, to close the lids of day,
> On drowsy wing proceed;

While chickering crickets, tremulous and long,
    Light's farewell inly heed,
    And give it parting song.

Chickering, more usually chicking, is used of clocks and seeds rattling in pods. Watchet must have survived in the cottages which Clare knew long after lexicography had written it off. Perhaps it still does. Presumably Watchet on the coast of Exmoor refers to the colour of the Bristol Channel in sunlight. This from a friendly fisherman, 'The dark watchet is one of the most famous of Yorkshire trout-flies and imitates the iron-blue dun. Its wings are made of the darkish blue feather from a tom-tit's tail.'

WILDERNESS

G. K. CHESTERTON once observed that so simple a line from the nursery as 'Over the hills and far away' is one of the most beautiful in all English poetry. The analyst will probably be right in assigning its magic to the roll of the 'r's and the final plaintive force of the 'w'. The same combination of 'r' and 'w' has the same poignancy in wilderness and bewilder. The latter word has lost its original conception of losing a person or being lost in a desolate place; bewilderments are now problems and puzzles of the mind. Few, if any, moderns, having strayed in the wilds, would describe themselves as bewildered, but wilderness has retained its territorial meaning as well as its mournful loveliness of sound. None knew the tricks of the poet's trade better than Fitzgerald (of *Omar*) and his

    Wilderness were Paradise enow

played memorably on the 'w's and 'r's. The young Shakespeare of 'Titus Andronicus' called Rome 'a wilderness of tigers', thus anticipating his better known 'wilderness of monkeys'. This last well describes a scamper of 'film-fans' to touch the garment of some well-featured nit-wit. Yet wilderness, an exquisite word, is really too good for anything but a desirable desert.

WILLOW

N o stranger, certainly, but deserving an obeisance. Ever since the
Jewish exile hung his harp thereon, ever since it was the parasol of
Behemoth ('The shady trees cover him with their shadow: the
willows of the brook compass him about'), it has been as much the
poet's joy as the symbol of mourning and of melancholy. It both
weeps and bewitches. 'Sing, willow, willow, willow.' Always it
sings. Why does Viola cry 'Make me a willow cabin at your gate'
when any other timber would do as well, and no doubt better, to
provide the building material for patient adoration? Try the line
with some other tree or timber, 'Make me an oaken cabin at your
gate'. The spell vanishes. There is usually some magic about the
letter 'w' when carefully employed. (I have alluded to the emotional difference between farewell and good-bye.) Alter 'Oh withered
is the garland of the war' into 'Oh faded is the garland of the fight'
and all is lost. Most lovely letter. Willow is its beneficiary, and
deserves to be, so lovely is the tree, in all its forms, not least the
Salyx Babylonica, the weeping willow. ·

WOODBINE

I n the note on Margarine I spoke of the ruin brought by science
and commerce to a word of pearly origin and charm. An interesting but melancholy roll might be called of words which have
suffered a similar fate: marmalade, which ought in accuracy to be
the essence of quinces, and the fragrant woodbine would be at the
top of the list. Woodbine has now gone up in smoke. But it has a
melting beauty if we can put the tobacconist out of mind. The
dictionaries usually equate woodbine with honeysuckle, but to
Shakespeare these two were man and wife: not one person. Everybody knows about Oberon's thymy bank 'quite over-canopied with
wild woodbine', but there is an even lovelier reference in the same
play:

So doth the woodbine the sweet honeysuckle
Gently entwist: the female ivy so
Enrings the barky fingers of the elm.

What a master of unostentatious alliteration was Shakespeare! The magic of these lines owes so much to the subtle interplay of e's and f's, of g's and r's.

WORTHY

THE adjective is unexciting, but the noun 'a worthy' has a good history. At one time it referred exclusively to an agreed and neatly balanced team of nine ancient heroes. There were three Jews, Joshua, David, and Judas Maccabaeus, three Gentiles, Hector, Alexander, and Julius Caesar, and three Christians, Arthur, Charlemagne, and Geoffrey of Bouillon. The admission of the last rather suggests the final and despairing choice of a cricket secretary, who is still in difficulties about raising a side at 1 p.m. on Saturday and is 'fairly in the Bouillon', as Mr. Wodehouse's Mr. Wooster so often remarks. But there seem to have been permissible variations. For example, when the clowns in *Love's Labour's Lost* present the Nine Worthies in mummery for the courtiers' entertainment, some of the above have dropped out and Hercules and Pompey have 'muscled in' to the honorific list.

Worthy next became the title of any man of note. It did not imply any ethical respectability. There is a nice Victorian volume of county lore called *The Worthies of Bucks*. One of the most ancient of these was the British King Cymbeline, who might be described as the earliest-known tenant of Chequers, since the fine, barrowed crest behind the Premier's seat is called Cymbeline's Mount and the village below has remained for ever Kimble. A much later and most 'desartless' worthy of these beechwoods was Sir Francis Dashwood. This landed Georgian playboy confessed that all numbers over four figures were to him impenetrable territory, but he was elevated (in the Age of Reason) to be Chancellor of the Exchequer, despite his bland assurance that any Budget of his would be received with ridicule. He was right. It was. So the Worthy retired to the more congenial activities of the Hellfire Club and to a private life of agreeable depravity.

WRITHEN AND WRITHLED

IN Kipling's poem on 'Sussex' in *The Five Nations*, we are told with as much melody as truth,

> No tender-hearted garden crowns,
>   No bosomed woods adorn
> Our blunt, bow-headed whale-backed Downs
>   But gnarled and writhen thorn.

Kipling's 'writhen' trees upon the Sussex hills are vivid to the eye, toughly invading and interrupting the smoothness of that curving line which Belloc deemed 'so noble and so bare'. Shakespeare, or whoever wrote *Henry VI*, Part I, had the same kind of twisty thing in mind when he used the word 'writhled'. But he applied it to a smaller matter.

> It cannot be this weak and writhled shrimp
> Should strike such terror to his enemies.

Were shrimps on sale in the fish-shops of his London so that he could note their writhled nature in a street stroll, or had he met the article alive and writhling while on a sea-side jaunt? But sea-side jaunts were unusual then. Shakespeare's marine contacts are strange and worth investigation.

YARE AND YERK

OUR Tudor revivalists ply us with warming-pans and half-timbered suburban villas, Ye Olde Gifte Shoppes, and God-wottery garden ornaments. Why not attend to the vocabulary, from which so many good and genuine Tudorisms are allowed to vanish? There is nothing bogus about yerk. It means, in the first place, to pull tight threads or laces, as a Ouida heroine might have yerked her corsets while her Guardsman did the same for his boots. But by Ouida's time the nice little, tight little word had disappeared. Its second meaning was to thrust or strike. Iago thought to have yerk'd Brabantio under the ribs and at Agincourt the wounded steeds of the French knights were seen to

> Fret fetlock deep in gore and with wild rage
> Yerk out their armed heels at their dead masters,
> Killing them twice.

Yerkers may be said to have done the job yarely. Yare for quick or nimble is another Tudor loss. Cleopatra, robed, crowned, and marble-constant to her death-wish, bade her attendant Iras be yare in giving her the asp and then yerked the venomous worm into her bosom. True, Shakespeare did not use the word yerk here, but yare has its immortal place in the greatest scene, as I believe, that Shakespeare ever wrote. For me there is nothing in English poetry to equal the last two acts of *Antony and Cleopatra*: in them the most ordinary words are yerked into glory or raised to a higher power, as mathematicians may say. In this book I have dealt mainly with words curious and beautiful in themselves. But genius in writing is an infinite capacity for making dim words shine and for giving to a commonplace collection of syllables new meaning and new magic.